COLLECTED POEMS
1956-1976

COLLECTED POEMS
1956-1976

David Wagoner

Indiana University Press / BLOOMINGTON & LONDON

Published in Canada by Fitzhenry & Whiteside Limited,
Don Mills, Ontario
Manufactured in the United States of America

Library of Congress Cataloging in Publication Data

Wagoner, David.
  Collected poems (1956–1976)

  I. Title.
PS3545.A345A17   1976   811'5'4   75-28915
ISBN 0-253-11245-1   1 2 3 4 5 80 79 78 77 76

These are all for Patt
with enduring love

ACKNOWLEDGMENTS

The poems from *A Place to Stand, The Nesting Ground, Staying Alive, New and Selected Poems, Riverbed,* and *Sleeping in the Woods* appeared originally in the following periodicals: *Poetry, Botteghe Oscure, New World Writing, New Poems, The New Yorker, The Hudson Review, International Literary Annual, Saturday Review, The London Observer, The Massachusetts Review, Prairie Schooner, Choice, Southern Review, Minnesota Review, Yale Review, Northwest Review, Seattle Magazine, Poetry Northwest, The Nation, The Journal of Creative Behavior, Chicago Review, Kayak, Harper's, Tri-quarterly, Shenandoah, The New Republic, The Iowa Review, Mademoiselle, Inside Outer Space, The American Scholar, Antaeus, Pebble, Hearse, Crazy Horse, Poetry Now, The Mill Mountain Review, The Kansas City Star, Western Humanities Review, The Ohio Review, American Review, Salmagundi, Monmouth Review,* and *The Virginia Quarterly Review.*

The new poems in this book appeared originally in the following periodicals in the years shown: "How Stump Found His Village," "How Stump Became Rock's Brother," "How Stump Dreamed of Earthmaker," 1974, VIRGINIA QUARTERLY REVIEW; "Song for the Painting of the Dead," "Song for the Eating of Barnacles," "Song for the Stealing of a Spring," "Song for Snake," "Song for the Skull of Black Bear," "Song for Ice," "Song for the Bones of Salmon," 1975, and "How Moss Grew Strong," "How Stone Held His Breath," "How Stump Fished in the Black River," 1976, POETRY NOW; "Travelling Light," "Tracking," "Walking in a Swamp," "Breaking Camp," "Roles," "Being Shot," "Walking at Night," "The Breaking Point," 1975, POETRY; "Who Shall Be the Sun?" 1974, THE IOWA REVIEW; "Beauty and the Beast," 1974, WESTERN HUMANI-

TIES REVIEW; "The Change," "From Here to There," 1975, NORTHWEST REVIEW; "The First Trick," "The Uncanny Illusion of the Headless Lady," 1975, KAYAK; "Song Against the Sky," "Song for a Stolen Soul," 1975, AMERICAN POETRY REVIEW; "Missing the Trail," "For a Thirteenth Anniversary," 1975, CHICAGO REVIEW; "Relics," 1976, NEW LETTERS; "The Death of Paul Bunyan," "Meeting a Bear," 1975, SOUTHERN REVIEW; "For Patt, Whispering to a Burro," 1976, THE HUDSON REVIEW; "At Low Tide," "The Old Words," 1976, POETRY MISCELLANY; "The Return of Icarus," 1976, TRIQUARTERLY. The following new poems appeared originally in THE NEW YORKER: "How Stump Stood in the Water," "Clancy," "Waiting in a Rain Forest," "Her Dream."

CONTENTS

from STAYING ALIVE (1966)

from SLEEPING IN THE WOODS *(1974)*

NEW POEMS *(1976)*

1

2

3

4

COLLECTED POEMS
1956-1976

TO MY FRIEND WHOSE PARACHUTE
DID NOT OPEN

Thrown backwards first, head over heels in the wind
Like solid streamers from the wing to tail,
You counted whatever pulses came to mind—
The black, the bright—and at the third, you pulled,
Pulled savagely at the ring clenched in your hand.

Down the smooth slope of your trajectory,
Obeying physics like a bauble of hail,
Thirty-two feet per second per second hurled
Toward treetops, cows, and crouching gravity
From the unreasonable center of the world,

You saw the cords trail out from behind your back,
Rise up and stand, tied to a piece of cloth
Whose edges wobbled, but would not spread wide
To borrow a cup of air and hold you both.
O that tall shimmer whispered you were dead.

You outraced thought. What good was thinking then?
Poor time—no time for plunging into luck
Which had, like your whirling, weightless flesh, grown thin.
I know angelic wisdom leaped from your mouth,
But not in words, for words can be afraid:

You sang a paean at the speed of sound,
Compressed miraculous air within your head
And made it fountain upward like a cowl.
And if you didn't, then you struck the ground.
And if you struck the ground, both of us died.

WORDS ABOVE A NARROW ENTRANCE

The land behind your back
Ends here: never forget
Signpost and weathercock
That turned always to point
Directly at your eyes;
Remember slackening air
At the top of the night,
Your feet treading on space.
The stream, like an embrace,
That swamped you to the throat
Has altered now; the briar
Rattling against your knees,
The warlock in disguise,
The giant at the root—
The country that seemed
Malevolence itself
Has gone back from the heart.

Beyond this gate, there lies
The land of the different mind,
Not honey in the brook,
None of the grass you dreamed.
Foresee water on fire,
And notches in a cloud;
Expect noise from a rock,
And faces falling apart.
The pathway underfoot,
Heaving its dust, will cross
A poisonous expanse
Where light knocks down the trees,
And whatever spells you took
Before, you will take anew
From the clack in the high wind.
Nothing will be at ease,
Nothing at peace, but you.

"TAN TA RA, CRIES MARS . . ."

—Thomas Weelkes

"Clang!" goes the high-framed, feather-tufted gong. The mace
And halberd, jostled together, ring on the cobblestones,
While straight with the horde, blue flies and pieces of wings
Sail to the war. Owl's egg in mouth, the prophet sings
Glory from thumb-stirred entrails, glory from eagle-stains
And smoke, holding a cup of moly to his face.

"Blat!" go the thin-stemmed silver horns. High-tail and
     horse-behind,
Prouder than bustles, rise in the streets to prank
And fidget with the air. See, plumes at their ears,
The unicorns stumble—the ram-horned bugbears,
And the spears, all brassily crested, rank on jack-straw rank,
And the phalanx of bellies, and the rusty, bellying wind.

"Tan Ta Ra!" cries Mars, last in the callithumpian line
Where midgets, riding on dogs, squeak like his chariot wheels
And weep. Ta Ra to his majesty's knotted thighs and fists!
The knuckle-browed, crotch-guarded master of hosts,
The raggedy-hafted Mars goes forth, with stars on his heels,
To battle, twitching our dust behind him like a gown.

SPRING SONG

O marvelous, our brave delight,
The sun stands in its hole,
And a warrior with a crocus wreath
Goes dancing for his soul,
Trailed closely by a harridan
Leading a milky cow.
Sigh, sigh for our lady,
The Mother of Fragments, now.

Delicate, on their hands and knees
Come Some from upper floors,
Leaping like hoppers, clocks, and toads
To celebrate all fours,
And twelve pocked maidens behind masks
Sing "Cuckolds All A-row."
Sigh, sigh for our lady,
The Mother of Fragments, now.

"I find no darkness in my head,
Alas," cries Bumbling Bill;
"O shake hands with the unenjoyed,"
Says lofty Mirabel.
"Simmer," sings the nightingale;
"Hokum," says the crow.
Sigh, sigh for our lady,
The Mother of Fragments, now.

"I dreamed that I was dead and gone,
Thank God," says Aunty Ann;
"Winter is over! Fold the beds,
And booze," cries Everyman.
"Bees," remarks the lily fly;
"Birdies," says the sow.
Sigh, sigh for our lady,
The Mother of Fragments, now.

O marvelous, O marvelous,
The widow of the weeds
Remembers feather, sun, and coast,
And plaits her bun with seeds,

And all the couriers of flesh
Snaffle themselves anew.
Sigh, sigh for our lady,
The Mother of Fragments, now.

THE FEAST

Maimed and enormous in the air,
The bird fell down to us and died.
Its eyelids were like cleats of fire,
And fire was pouring from its side.

Beneath the forest and the ash
We stood and watched it. Beak to breast,
It floundered like a dying fish,
Beating its wings upon the dust.

What vague imbalance in our hearts
Leaned us together then? The frost
Came feathered from a sky of quartz;
Huge winter was our holy ghost.

O for light's sake, we turned to see
Waterglass forming on a stone;
A hag laughed under every tree;
The trees came slowly toppling down,

And all of the staring eyes were false.
Our jaws unhinged themselves, grew great,
And then we knelt like animals
To the body of this death, and ate.

THE MAN FROM THE TOP OF THE MIND

From immaculate construction to half death,
See him: the light bulb screwed into his head,
The vacuum tube of his sex, the electric eye.
What lifts his foot? What does he do for breath?

His nickel steel, oily from neck to wrist,
Glistens as though by sunlight where he stands.
Nerves bought by the inch and muscles on a wheel
Spring in the triple-jointed hooks of his hands.

As plug to socket, or flange along a beam,
Two become one; yet what is he to us?
We cry, "Come, marry the bottom of our minds.
Grant us the strength of your impervium."

But clad in a seamless skin, he turns aside
To do the tricks ordained by his transistors—
His face impassive, his arms raised from the dead,
His switch thrown one way into animus.

Reach for him now, and he will flicker with light,
Divide preposterous numbers by unknowns,
Bump through our mazes like a genius rat,
Or trace his concentric echoes to the moon.

Then, though we beg him, "Love us, hold us fast,"
He will stalk out of focus in the air,
Make gestures in an elemental mist,
And falter there—as we will falter here

When the automaton pretends to dream
And turns in rage upon our horrible shapes—
Those nightmares, trailing shreds of his netherworld,
Who must be slaughtered backward into time.

MURDER MYSTERY

After the murder, like parades of Fools,
The bungling supernumeraries come,
Sniffing at footprints, looking under rugs,
Clasping the dead man with prehensile tools.
Lens against nose, false beard down to his knees,
The Hawkshaw enters, hoists his bag of tricks,
And passes out suspicion like lemonade:
"Where were you when the victim—" "In my room."
"Didn't you ask him whether—" "Double locks."
"Who switched the glasses on the—" "Crippled legs."
"Why were the ballroom curtains—" "Mad for years."
Then, tripping on clues, they wander through the house,
And search each other, frighten themselves with guns,
Ransack the kitchen and the sherry bins,
And dance in the bushes with the cats and dogs.

"Where is he?" says the Captain. "Nobody cares."
"We did it!" scream the butler and the maid.
"I did it too!" the jolly doctor cries.
And all join in—detective, counterfoil,
Ingénue, hero, and the family ghosts—
And, flapping like tongues, the trapdoors babble guilt,
The window-boxes, closets understairs,
Whatnots and chandeliers, grandfather clocks,
The sealed-up attic with its litter of bones—
All of them shake, and pour their secrets out.
And the happy party, bearing aloft the dead,
Handcuffed and drunk, go singing toward the jail;
Stage-hands roll up their sleeves, fold up the lawn,
Dismantle the hedges and the flowerbed,
Then follow, hauling the mansion, to confess.
Meanwhile, in another place—their figures cold,
Both turned to shadows by a single pain,
Bloodless together—the killer and the slain
Have kissed each other in the wilderness,
Touching soft hands and staring at the world.

MEMENTO MORI

In my list of choices, death had not appeared.
The forest in my head, the scrambling words,
The stars and motes behind my eyes grew fierce
And fearsome before sleep. But none were black.
None loomed. In the woods were only birds to be feared;
In words, their loss; in stars, their merciless swords.
By the praise of my flesh, I could always pierce,
With clean ferocity, sleep's cul-de-sac.

I moved through the flaking air and had my say.
Time held its mirrors to my face: I looked,
And nose to nose, I stared my image down.
The rout of cretinous horrors in the night
Had left me cold but steady in my day.
What if the light was huge and steep? I knocked
Out of pride against the sun and dune
To make them speak. They did. I took no fright.

Angels and ashes seemed the freaks of age.
"Bring out your dead," I cried, and cocked my eye
To see the hillocks and the loam-beds stir.
Earth held. No bone broke out. No head of death
Sprang like a comet from the world at large,
Trailing its dark. "Poets refuse to die,"
I wrote on stone. Yet now, O God in Thy blur,
Who is it stuffs this murdering dust in my breath?

LULLABY THROUGH THE SIDE
OF THE MOUTH

Goodnight, unlucky three. Mice at a feast
Go nibbling the grain away; the wrens
Fluff one another in the hollow post;
And moths are knuckling at the windowpanes.

O pray to the wall, pray to the billypan,
Render all praise to footboards and the sheets,
Call up the spiral mattress if you can:
But see, at your eyes, the counterclockwise lights.

Now you must sacrifice—first, to the dark,
Next, to the crippled underhalf of the mind—
Your faces, hearts, whatever does good work,
Before you come to the burrows at wit's end.

Once more, the holes lie open into dreams:
In one, a hairless tail; in one, a quill;
And, in a third, antennae with soft plumes.
Now put them on, dear Lust, my Love, poor Will.

May forefeet lift each kernel like a cup;
May beak and claw touch heaven under wings;
May the dust-flecked moth find every window up.
But those are joys. You will not dream such things.

THE FIRST WORD

There had been sounds before: the trumpeting snout,
The crackling of the earth.
The trees had spoken for a million years;
Water had fallen; the great bees, gesturing,

Droned in their hollows, crying what was sweet.
Deep in his cave, he heard them; and his throat
Clouded with shapes and storms.
What could he do, whose tongue was but a thing?

Was it death-noise first? Or the would-be thunderer,
Man become weather, shouting at the sky?
Or naked and hungry, mad, nibbling at fur,
The one who heard the Others growl as they bled,
And dreamed his terrible name?
Or did his fingers bring such bitterness
From world to lip
He cried aloud to see them come again?

The sunlight blazed outside, purple and green
On the stones and fern-leaves. Did he call it *day*?
No, but he raised his eyes.
The roof of his mouth was burning like the sun;
The water beneath his tongue had run away,
And Another stood at the entrance like a god.
A voice stirred in the wilderness of his head.
Was it *yes* or *no*? Was it *you* or *me* he said?

from
THE NESTING GROUND
(1963)

AFTER CONSULTING MY YELLOW PAGES

All went well today in the barbers' college:
The razor handles pointed gracefully outward,
The clippers were singing like locusts. And far away
On the fox farms, the red and silver sun brushed lightly
Tail after tail. Happily, the surveyors
Measured the downhill pasture through a theodolite,
Untroubled by birchtrees. The makers of fraternal regalia
Conceived a new star-burst, and the parakeet
In the green bird hospital was coaxed out of danger.
Business came flying out of the horse-meat market,
And under the skillful world, the conduits groped
Forward, heavy with wires, to branch at the lake.
Fish brokers prodded salmon on the walloping dock.
The manifold continuous forms and the luminous
        products
Emerged, endlessly shining, while the cooling towers
Poured water over themselves like elephants.
Busily the deft hands of the locksmith and wig-maker
In basement and loft, in the magnifying light,
Turned at their labors. The universal joints,
Hose-couplings, elastic hosiery, shingles and shakes,
The well-beloved escrow companies, the
        heat-exchangers,
Bead-stringers, makers of disappearing beds,
The air-compressors randy with oxygen—
All sprang, remarkably, out of the swinging doors.

And where were you? What did you do today?

•

DIARY

At Monday dawn, I climbed into my skin
And went to see the money. There were the shills:
I conned them—oh, the coins fell out of their mouths,
And paint peeled from the walls like dollar bills.
Below their money-belts, I did them in.

All day Tuesday, grand in my underwear,
I shopped for the world, bought basements and airplanes,
Bargained for corners and pedestrians
And, when I'd marketed the elms away,
Swiped from the water, stole down to the stones.

Suddenly Wednesday offered me my shirt,
Trousers, and shoes. I put them on to dream
Of the one-way stairway and the skittering cloud,
Of the dangerous, footsore crossing at the heart
Where trees, rivers, and stones reach for the dead.

And the next day meant the encircling overcoat
Wherein I sweltered, woolly as a ram:
From butt to swivel, I hoofed it on the loam,
Exacting tribute from the flock in the grass.
My look passed through the werewolf to the lamb.

Friday shied backwards, pulling off my clothes:
The overcoat fell open like a throat;
Shirt-tail and shoe went spidery as a thought,
And covetous drawers whipped knee-deep in a knot.
My skin in a spiral tapered into gold.

And it was naked Saturday for love
Again: the graft grew milky at a kiss.
I lay on the week with money, lust, and vapor,
Megalomania, fear, the tearing-off,
And love in a coil. On Sunday, I wrote this.

CLOSING TIME

At midnight, flaking down like chromium
Inside the tavern, light slips off the bar
And tumbles in our laps. The tumbler falling
Off the edge of the table goes to pieces
As quick as mercury around our shoes.
Goodnight to shuffleboard and counter-check.
The last ball-bearing pins its magnet down
And sinks into a socket like the moon.

Over the rings around our eyes, the clock
Says time to decipher wives, husbands, and cars
On keychains swinging under bleary light.
Goodnight to folding friends on the parking lot
As parallel as windows in a wallet.
Lined up like empties on the curb, goodnight
To all who make the far side of the street,
Their eyelids pressed as tight as bottlecaps.

Goodnight to those with jacks as openers,
Those whose half-cases chill their pelvises,
And those with nothing on tap all day tomorrow
Who wind up sleeping somewhere cold as stars,
Who make the stairs and landings, but not doors,
Those in the tubs, or hung on banisters,
Those with incinerators in their arms,
Whose mouths lie open for another one.

Goodnight to drivers driven by themselves
To curve through light years at the straightaway.
Goodnight to cloverleaf and yellow-streak,
To all those leading sheriff's deputies
Over soft shoulders into power-poles,
The red-in-the-face whose teeth hang down by nerves,
The far-afield, the breakers of new ground
Who cartwheel out of sight, end over end.

A GUIDE TO DUNGENESS SPIT

Out of wild roses down from the switching road between
    pools
We step to an arm of land washed from the sea.
On the windward shore
The combers come from the strait, from narrows and shoals
Far below sight. To leeward, floating on trees
In a blue cove, the cormorants
Stretch to a point above us, their wings held out like
    skysails.
Where shall we walk? First, put your prints to the sea,
Fill them, and pause there:
Seven miles to the lighthouse, curved yellow-and-grey
    miles
Tossed among kelp, abandoned with bleaching rooftrees,
Past reaches and currents;
And we must go afoot at a time when the tide is heeling.
Those whistling overhead are Canada geese;
Some on the waves are loons,
And more on the sand are pipers. There, Bonaparte's gulls
Settle a single perch. Those are sponges.
Those are the ends of bones.
If we cross to the inner shore, the grebes and goldeneyes
Rear themselves and plunge through the still surface,
Fishing below the dunes
And rising alarmed, higher than waves. Those are
    cockleshells.
And these are the dead. I said we would come to these.
Stoop to the stones.
Overturn one: the grey-and-white, inch-long crabs come
    pulsing
And clambering from their hollows, tiptoeing sideways.
They lift their pincers
To defend the dark. Let us step this way. Follow me closely
Past snowy plovers bustling among sand-fleas.
The air grows dense.   ·
You must decide now whether we shall walk for miles and
    miles
And whether all birds are the young of other creatures
Or their own young ones,
Or simply their old selves because they die. One falls,

And the others touch him webfoot or with claws,
Treading him for the ocean.
This is called sanctuary. Those are feathers and scales.
We both go into mist, and it hooks behind us.
Those are foghorns.
Wait, and the bird on the high root is a snowy owl
Facing the sea. Its flashing yellow eyes
Turn past us and return;
And turning from the calm shore to the breakers, utterly
    still,
They lead us by the bay and through the shallows,
Buoy us into the wind.
Those are tears. Those are called houses, and those are
    people.
Here is a stairway past the whites of our eyes.
All our distance
Has ended in the light. We climb to the light in spirals,
And look, between us we have come all the way,
And it never ends
In the ocean, the spit and image of our guided travels.
Those are called ships. We are called lovers.
There lie the mountains.

THE NESTING GROUND

Piping sharp as a reed,
The small bird stood its ground
Twenty feet from ours.
From the shore, another answered
 (The piercing double note
Meant killdeer and killdeer)
And skimmed over the sand,
Over the sparse grass,
Lit, then scurried away,
Flopping, crooking its wing
To flash a jagged streak
And the amber of its back.

When the first bird moved a foot
And struck out at the air,
Two chicks leaped after it,
Their plain heads clear as day.
We walked straight to the spot,
Needing to stir what we love,
Knelt down and found nothing,
Not even when we stared
Each checkered, pebbly stalk
Into its own semblance.
We flattened disbelief
With the four palms of our hands.

But the grown birds broke themselves,
Crippled their cries and wings
So near us, we stood up
To follow their sacrifice
That tempts the nails of creatures
Who, needing flight, forget
Whatever they might have caught
By standing still instead.
We kept on walking, led
By pretended injuries,
Till we were far away,
Then turned, as the birds turned
To sail back to the source
Where we had touched our knees,

And saw through our strongest glass
The young spring out of cover,
Piping one death was over.

HOMAGE

When broken laughter broke
From the edge of a bough
I turned, and a buzzing went
Bushes and yards away
Like a shot and disappeared,
Then quick came humming back
To hang like a red hook
First of all in the air
Embedded in a blur,
Then instantly nowhere.
I glanced from marsh to creek,
To the arches of my eyes
And found flush in the sun
The striking hummingbird
Whirring and chortling down
Faster than I could follow
Within a foot of my ear
Vanishing there and there
Only to reappear
Forty feet aloft,
Unsteady and permanent,
Transfixed, then gone again
To slant straight at my head
But missing, rocketing by.
A streak of redness left
Behind it like a stroke
Bent me down in half,
Bowing me toward its mate
As drab as a burnt leaf
Perched silent at my elbow.

SÉANCE FOR TWO HANDS

When all the shades could spell
On slates as though at school
Or rap on the wall,
Life was doing well.
Out of the cracks in marble,
From under the lifted table
Came the shape of the soul:
The wind in a shirt-tail,
A fish in a white veil,
The moon behind an owl.
Though put to bed with a shovel
The body like a wheel
Rose from its rut at will
Nor kept the spirit level.

But the dead no longer press
Against the looking-glass.
They have gone out of the gauze,
Away from the feet of yews;
Their lips no longer pause
At the edges of lilies.
Disenthralled from cats' eyes,
Battered from the cows,
Dropped from the breasts of crows,
Driven from the flies,
The ghosts of the latter days
Of the soul's progress
Needle a point in space.
Death alone haunts our house.

THE EMERGENCY MAKER

"Still alive—" the message ran,
Tapped on a broken rail—
"The air is somewhere else, the shaft
Is blacker than the coal.
Lower a light and break the rock

That plugged this bloody hole."
But I, who had tossed the dynamite,
Had better things to do
Than juggle stones from here to there
Or bring the dark to day.
Go shovel yourself and hold your nose:
The diggers have to die.

"We'll starve in a week—" the radio said,
Fading in salty weather—
"We've eaten kelp and canvas shoes,
Played at father and mother,
And now we've run out of things to do
To seaweed and each other."
But I, who had drained their compass oil,
Had better fish to fry
Than those I'd caught in a wet canoe
Or over my father's knee.
Go down to the sea and drink your fill:
The lubbers have to die.

"For God's sake—" said the heliograph
High on the mountaintop—
"We're frozen quick on a narrow ledge:
If you want us down, come up.
The avalanche slopes above our heads
Like a nose over a lip."
But I, who had cut their ropes in half,
Gone tumbling down the scree,
Stuffed the crevasse with edelweiss,
And pointed the wrong way,
Said *Pull up your boots and take the air:*
We climbers have to die.

FREE PASSAGE

Come away, my sea-lane baggage,
For a crack at the sky.
Come with me in an armlock over the ocean, my china
    breakage,
We shall go everywhere in a day, grant liberty, squeak, and
    never die.

From docks to lavender palaces,
Oh what comings and goings, my rattan May basket!
Adored as we fall through tissue-paper, through balconies,
    fountains, and trellises,
We shall be borne up like desserts in cream, stuffed like a
    brisket,

And spun in the air like platters.
At concerts, we shall arrive in all three aisles at once, be
    lionized in jungles, horsed at the seaside.
Chairmen on tiptoe and the giddy, sidelong doctors
Will toast us and be irrevocably toasted.

I have initialed everything, bought floating flashlights,
Filled my binocular flasks with the hottest chutney.
Bye, Mommy! Bye, Daddy! Bye, Sissy! Bye-bye, Fatso!
I'm salting off on the briny with my candy.

Oh my snifter, my tumble-rick, sweet crank of the stars,
My banjo-bottomed, fretful girl,
Tear off those swatches of silk, your hems and haws, and
    coil them up like streamers—
Get set to toss them over the bounding rail.

Sal volatile! Coral uplift! Oh my pink receiver! Freely I
    swear
Our tanglefoot Rosicrucian wedding on a gangplank,
    among the hoots and the spouting fireboats,
Above flashbulbs, fish-heads, and the drowning divers,
Will be as immortal as rats.

THE CALCULATION

A man six feet tall stands on a curb, facing a light sus-
pended fifteen feet above the middle of a street thirty feet
wide. He begins to walk along the curb at five m.p.h. After
he has been walking for ten seconds, at what rate is the
length of his shadow increasing?

—a problem given by my calculus instructor,
Penn State, 1946

Facing a streetlight under batty moths
And June bugs ratcheting like broken clock-springs,
I stand, for the sake of a problem, on the curb—
Neither in grass nor gutter—while those wings
Switch down the light and patch my undershirt.

I turn half-right. My shadow cuts a hedge,
Climbs through a rhododendron to a porch,
And nods on a windowsill. How far it goes
I leave to burglars and Pythagoras.
Into the slanting glare I slant my watch,

Then walk five miles per hour, my shoes on edge
In a practiced shuffle past the sewer grid
Over the gold no-parking-or-pausing zones
And into the clear—five seconds—into dirt,
Then over a sawhorse studded with lanterns,

And at the tenth I stiffen like a stump
Whose lopped head ripples with concentric figures,
Note the location of my other head
In a garden, but keep trundling forward,
Ignoring *Doppelgängers* from moon and lawn-lamp,

My eyes alert now, leveling my feet,
Seeing my shadow sweeping like a scythe
Across the stalks of daisies, barking trees,
And scraping up the blistered weatherboard
To the eaves of houses, scaling the rough shingles.

At fifteen seconds, in a vacant lot,
My head lies on a board. I count it off.
I think back to the garden, and I guess,

Instructor, after fifteen years of sweat,
It was increasing five feet plus per second.

At the start, I could have fallen, turned around,
Or crossed to the very center of confusion,
My shadow like a manhole, no one's length,
Or the bulb itself been broken with a shot,
And all my reckoning have gone unreckoned.

But I was late because my shadow was
Pointing toward nothing like the cess of light,
Sir, and bearing your cold hypotenuse—
That cutter of corners, jaywalker of angles—
On top of my head, I walked the rest of the night.

ELEGY FOR SIMON CORL, BOTANIST

With wildflowers bedded in his mind,
My blind great-uncle wrote a book.
His lips and beard were berry-stained,
Wrist broken like a shepherd's crook.

His door leaned open to the flies,
And May, like tendrils, wandered in.
The earth rose gently to his knees;
The clouds moved closer than his skin.

Sun against ear, he heard the slight
Stamen and pistil touch for days,
Felt pollen cast aslant like light
Into the shadows of his eyes.

When autumn stalked the leaves, he curled;
His fingers ripened like the sky;
His ink ran to a single word,
And the straight margin went awry.

When frost lay bristling on the weeds,
He smoothed it with a yellow thumb,
Followed his white cane to the woods
Between the saxifrage and thyme,

And heard the hornets crack like ice,
Felt worms arch backward in the snow;
And while the mites died under moss,
The clean scar sang across his brow.

OFFERTORY

Ready to leave for work, I look around
To check windows and switches: in the sink,
A pool of coffee poured from the last cup
Gleams near the drain; the ring in the bath
At its own level holds my body up;
And crumpled on the bed, blankets like sheep
Crouch where the ram came, reeling, from his dip.
So many rituals: two cups for the gods
Of the left and right temple, the grounds gone
Where all libations go; on porcelain,
My yesterday in an upright, shrinking lather;
Dial down and ticking under the pillow-slip,
Two sheets to the wind hauled back from sleep—
I leave these for the maker of light whose rain
On the alarming morning fell again.

PLUMAGE

Beside a bush, the pheasant on one foot
Is standing motionless, green head erect,
Bronze belly feathers washing into grass.
He stares to know me. Staring back, I see
Each wing-bar tasselled like a shock of wheat,
The tail grained edgewise, shoulders flaking white,
His buff flank strewn with black, a scarlet cheek
Cupped to an eye-spot like a flowerhead.

But where? He falls to pieces in my eye—
To flinders, flaws of intersecting light
Where dust and the veins of leaves are cancelled out,
Cross-hatched and baffled at the edge of sight—
And pours all distance forward through a speck
Till stalk and stick, spikelet and ripe seed
Go hedging back as one in the hedgerow.
Too carelessly, I take another breath.

Out of the shadows, booming, rocketing,
Shaking direction, breaking left and right,
The pheasant clappers upward, leaves behind
Nothing in amber, neither claw nor strut,
No gaping side, no parcel of a wing
Clipped off by birdshot as a proof of death.
Flashing across a gully up the wind,
Again, he drops to pieces in the sun.

ONCE UPON A PICNIC GROUND

Once upon a picnic ground
Our love was in the bag,
And bread and butter by the pound
Was easily ours to beg.
The nancy boys and gutter girls
Fell over themselves to fetch
The hard-boiled eggs and carrot curls
We needed in the clutch.

And twice upon a picnic ground
Our love lay on the table.
Whenever we passed our plates around,
It gave us heaps of trouble:
Up from our pot of boston beans
Molasses overflowed
And, sticking against our hotdog buns,
Undid the work of God.

When these events were stuffed, we found
Our bag was full of shells,
And ginger bears, without a sound,
Came in their hairy shawls
Through sweet incinerator smoke—
Their muzzles caked with crumbs—
To budge us out of the way and make
A bed for stumblebums.

Now robber jays and pheasant hens
Cry from the hemlock tree
Above the streaming garbagecans
For my lost love and me.
Their craws are full of lightning-bugs;
Their molting feathers cross
On bottles, bags, and bearskin rugs,
And the enduring grass.

NO SALE

Shushing their ankle dogs,
The women behind doors
In curlers, saying No,
All wore their lipstick thin,
Waited till I would go,
Then latched themselves back in.

At the corner in his car
The siding salesman said,
"A high-class canvasser
Tickles them through the screen.
Look them straight in the chest.
Quit telling the truth."

And after pounding weeks
Through showers and heat-waves
At a glance I knew the worst
Weatherboards and shakes
Or paint like blistered heels.
By hundreds of yards and stairs

I talked to all the wives
Who leaned on shaky walls.
I said an engineer
Was waiting at their pleasure
To insulate their sides,
To hold their windows up.

I slummed them, saying floors
Would warp them out of place.
Get ready to play house
Like cards, as serious
As mothers playing trumps.
What else can save your face?

I said a house needs skin
Thicker than powder-base
To stop the sagging, keep
The plaster in its cast,
Packed around bones for years.
But nothing turned their heads.

Swindled by someone else,
They sat in curls all day,
Waiting to be let down,
Waiting to fall straight
And stringy at midnight.
So I went straight, and quit.

THE BREATHING LESSON

"Sensations of smell are relatively homogeneous and un-
translatable into the form of language. Nobody can en-
large upon an odor."

—Oscar W. Firkins

Around the compass, soap-flakes and burnt corn,
A swamp, the acid cracked from boiling oil,
Sulfur dioxide, plumage of soft coal,
The yellow wreckage of Lake Michigan—
The unpredictable first breath of a day
Where I grew up depended on the wind.

My life would turn tail like a weathervane
And find attention wrung out on the line,
My breath in dollops, dead frogs in the throat,
The drill in the forehead, branches of membrane
Flocking with soot, or the unhallowed dregs
Of the lake come lapping up like burlap dogs.

Led by the nose around the pit of self
In all directions, I was washerwoman,
The dying year-god, infidel at the gate,
The egg of the world, machine-man, rancid goat.
But if the wind was veering, backing off,
They choked themselves on metamorphosis.

O Lux, Mazola, Wolf Lake, Standard Oil,
O city dump, O docks of Bethlehem—
Though a mind, run through its middle, can't forget
What creatures roamed its baffling passages,
In the dead calm of morning once, I rose
Breathless without your help, and walked away.

THE SATIRISTS

With verminous ringlets leaping on their wigs,
They staggered through the city, stuttering rage
At a world pulled inside out by hypocrites.
Lace to their elbows, elbows steeped in swill,
The carpet-knights answered like Latin-mongers;
The acrobats and prigs guffawed in the dark
To praise, like cats, the tickling end of the quill.

Oh indignation lit their cheeks like chilblains,
And while their gouty great-toes pulsed on the stones,
Gin Lane flocked out to chorus, "Up smocks all!"
Ambition rolled with Simony in the streets

Where life lay squeezed into its opposites.
"Reform!" they shouted, but their voices wheezed
Like drainpipes through an ever-thickening phlegm.
"Blindmen!" they cried, and jumped out of their shoes,
But still the pock-faced pimps gnawed at the moon.

Toasting themselves in black and yellow bile,
They turned splenetic wisdom to the wall,
Weeping for Donkeys and the City of Christ
Or country pleasures beaten into holes.
Those great, blood-let, exacerbated men—
Foredoomed to choke like thieves on their own
        tongues—
All muttered, "Cover your hearts and trim them close,"
While they lurched home to cork anonymous wives.

ADVICE TO THE ORCHESTRA

Start like pieces of string:
Lank homeliness attached, maybe, to nothing.
Then oh! my harpies, brush over the rows and thrust
Music like brooms under their chairs, rouse out the cats, the
    purses, and the dust.
Make them all leap up—the ophthalmic trance-breakers, the
    doggers, midge-killers, all the pie-faced gawkies and
    their crumbs.
Give them music to break their glasses, to knock their eyelids
    up like hatbrims.

When they run, follow them out of doors, out of windows,
Assault their tails with chorts and tootles, oompahs and
    glissandos.
Snare them. Give them no hiding places. Let them be draked
    in the reeds.
Slide after them into dumps and suburbs, over trembling
    hairpin roads,
Across channels and bays to the tilted islands where water
    whirls on edge.
Spiral through tunnels, over the baffling rocks and the spokes
    of forests, to the last desperate wheelprint, committing
    outrage.

Oh my outlandish ones,
Offer yourselves through the mold on brass, through skins
    and bones.
Your music must consume its instruments
Or die lost in the elbow-joints and valves, in snaggle and
    crook, ratchet and pinchbeck, in the folded winds.
Let the boom come. Send up the burning brows,
The white domes of your echoes.

Stand in the pit. Strike the sides of your death. Let spherical
    thunder
Rise from gravel-throated, unharmonious earth, the stricken
    center,
Beyond air fringed like a curtain, through the cabbage leaves
    and angels of the moon,
The mercurial archangels,—rise to untune

The principalities and powers, the squash of the sun, virtues
and jovial dominations, the saturnine thrones,
calliope-pumping cherubim and seraphim with their
heads ablaze
Against the old gods' mobile, eccentric knees.

OUT FOR A NIGHT

It was No, no, no, practicing at a chair,
And No at the wall, and one for the fireplace,
And down the stairs it was No over the railing,
And two for the dirt, and three Noes for the air,

And four in a row rapidly over the bar,
Becoming Maybe, Maybe, from spittoon to mirror,
It was shrugging cheeks on one face after another,
And Perhaps and So-So at both ends of a cigar,

Five, and it was Yes as a matter of fact
Who said it wasn't all the way down the bottle,
It was Hell Yes over and lightly underfoot,
And tongue like a welcome mat for t¹e bartender,

And Yes in the teeth, Yes like a cracked whistle,
And one for you, and two for the rest of us,
Indeed, Indeed, the chair got up on the table,
And Yes up on the chair and kissed the light

And the light burned, and Yes fell out of the chair,
And the chair slid off the table, and it was Maybe
All over the floor, tilted, it was squat,
And plunge to the rear, and smack lips like a baby,

It was five for the fingers Absolutely,
Four in the corners, it was three for the show,
And two descending eyebrows to make a ceiling,
And No to the knees and chin, and one Goodbye.

EVERY GOOD BOY DOES FINE

I practiced my cornet in a cold garage
Where I could blast it till the oil in drums
Boomed back; tossed free-throws till I couldn't move my
    thumbs;
Sprinted through tires, tackling a headless dummy.

In my first contest, playing a wobbly solo,
I blew up in the coda, alone on stage,
And twisting like my hand-tied necktie, saw the judge
Letting my silence dwindle down his scale.

At my first basketball game, gangling away from home
A hundred miles by bus to a dressing room,
Under the showering voice of the coach, I stood in a towel,
Having forgotten shoes, socks, uniform.

In my first football game, the first play under the lights
I intercepted a pass. For seventy yards, I ran
Through music and squeals, surging, lifting my cleats,
Only to be brought down by the safety man.

I took my second chances with less care, but in dreams
I saw the bald judge slumped in the front row,
The coach and team at the doorway, the safety man
Galloping loud at my heels. They watch me now.

You who have always horned your way through passages,
Sat safe on the bench while some came naked to court,
Slipped out of arms to win in the long run,
Consider this poem a failure, sprawling flat on a page.

THAT OLD GANG OF MINE

"Warden, I thank you." "Not at all." He bowed.
With my dress cane, I hit him on the head.

"A stirring evening, Officer." The guard
Blinked at my spinning watch-chain. Then he snored.

"Come out, good thieves," I whispered to the walls,
And heard the fine teeth mousing in the cells.

Sliding the key-ring under the cold bars,
I tiptoed down the hall and out of doors.

The first explosion coughed the windows out;
The second made stones generous to a fault;

The third threw up the prison, clapped its wings,
Squinted the lights, and pierced the sirens' lungs.

Over the rubble in their shredded suits,
Out of the tangle of bent license plates,

Through the dim ruckus between dust and guns,
Came my key men, the unlocked skeletons,

Bumping their knobby knees against the rocks
That once stood tall as hell to shepherd crooks.

"Run for our lives!" I whispered. "First comes grass,
Then shrubs, then trees, then water, and then grace."

Oscar the Bounder ripped his jacket off
And vaulted toward the deep night in the buff.

Phineas the Mouthpiece staggered, his eyes shut,
And hawked to break the thick years in his throat.

Sylvester the One-man Sack-race, self-possessed,
Stalked through the brambles, lofty as a post.

Esau the Actor, two feet, four feet, none,
Rose past the willows, flickered, and was gone.

Then out of the heap, the unpacked bloodhounds came
Groggy but eager, snuffling the old game.

Fit to be tied behind them, stumbling guards
Saw their long leashes snarling into braids

As we went crosspath, taking to our heels,
In five directions, tireless through the hills.

At dawn, across the water, over the dunes,
Past the bleak alders and the bleaker downs,

Over the thorn scrub like *cheval-de-frise*,
I went to meet them, purple with their praise,

And as we leaped and crowed in a shower of cash,
We danced a ring around the burning bush.

A DAY IN THE CITY

Dismounting from stools and benches, pouring through bars,
Let's do the day up brown,
Knock it back like a short drink, get off our trolley,
Put our foot downtown.

There, cutting the sun in half with our eyelids,
Sinister with love,
We shall wait till those feet, swollen to thousands on the
      pavement,
Are aching to move.

Then from the joints at our knees, the crooks at our elbows,
From all the hugging sides,
Through the calves and hams, the perpendicular marches
Will drill us into squads.

Rising from cornerstones, cripples with bristling pencils
Will jam on their caps
And join us—the floorwalkers and shoplifters, gulls and
      barkers,
The blindmen in their cups,

And the churruping children, the sailors and loaded Indians,
Fur-bearing stylish stouts,
All thronging from broken curb to curb and up the
      lamp-posts,
Onto ledges like goats.

And the city is ours. See, the bridges all give up, the arcades
Rattle their silver shops,
Buildings chip in, the sidewalks roll over like dogs, hotels
Chime their fire-escapes.

Here on a glittering carpet of plate glass go dancing
Till leggings and bandages
Trail us like trains round the fountain to the plaza, till our
      faces
Leap from our jaws,

And our sleeves roll back to the trombones and armbands,
And, shooting the mailchutes,
We stand in circles on every floor, shaking our palms,
Flagging our bedsheets.

We shall trump up a total noise, a silence battered
Like rams in the air.
Let the sewers hoot, all risers drop their treads
To the wrenched foot of the stair.

Then quietly, left and right, with our bandoliers
Crossed on our blouses,
We shall drift away through the empty business-ends of the
    streets
To go back to pieces,

While the city lets out the fiery-red, grumbling water-wagons
To lay the dust,
And sends toward our houses, through every alley,
The huge, defaced,

Skulking, familiar, handle-breaking, off-key garbageman
Who had been killed,
But who now heaps under the raised lids, our old lives
Before they are cold.

ON SEEING AN X-RAY OF MY HEAD

Now face to face, hard head, old nodder and shaker,
While we still have ears,
Accept my congratulations: you survived
My headlong blunders
As, night by night, my knuckles beat at your brow
More often than at doors,
Yet you were pampered, waved from the end of your
    stick
Like a bird in feathers,
Wrapped in towels, whistled and night-capped,
And pressed into pillows.
I see by this, the outline of our concern,
What you will lose
Before too long: the shadowy half of chin
And prodding nose,
Thatchwork of hair, loose tongue, and parting lips,
My look as blank as yours,
And yet, my madcap, catch-all rattlepot,
Nothing but haze
Shows on this picture what we had in mind,
The crannied cauliflower
Ready to boil away at a moment's notice
In a fit of vapors
And leave us holding the bag. Oh my brainpan,
When we start our separate ways
With opaque, immortal fillings clenched in our teeth
Like a bunch of keys,
And when your dome goes rolling into a ditch
And, slack in the jaws,
Stops at a hazard, some unplayable lie,
Accept at your ease
Directly what was yours at one remove:
Light through your eyes,
Air, dust, and water as themselves at last. Keep smiling.
Consider the source.
Go back to the start, old lime-pit, remembering flesh
    and skin,
Your bloody forebears.

STANDING HALFWAY HOME

At the last turn in the path, where locust thorns
Halter my sleeve, I suddenly stand still
For no good reason, planting both my shoes.
No other takes its place when my noise ends.
The hush is on. Through the deserted boughs,
Through fireweed, bracken, duff, down to the ground,
The air comes as itself without a sound
And deepens at my knees like waste of breath.

Behind my back lies the end of property;
Ahead, around a corner, a new house.
Barbed wire and aerials cross up and out
To mark the thresholds of man's common sense:
Keep out, keep talking. Doing neither one,
Here, central and inert, I stop my mouth
To reassure all the invisible
For whom my sight and sound were dangerous.

Eyes in the wings of butterflies stare through
The hazel leaves. Frozen beside my foot,
A tawny skink relaxes on its toes.
I shift my weight. The sun bears down the hill,
And overhead, past where an eye can turn,
A hiss of feathers parts the silence now.
At my arm's length a seedy, burr-sized wren,
As if I were a stalk, bursts into song.

THE OBSERVER

The woman kneeling by the side of the road
Sketches a porcupine lying dead,
Its tail on pavement, chest on the narrow shoulder.
The waxed face of the moon wears through the sky.
She turns a page and reaches out to touch
The quills left upright on the scruff of its neck.
Rising, she circles, and a car sweeps by:
The trailing wind goes past her, and the dust
Swerves to a standstill, hovers, and falls down.

For an hour, I've waited while the night sank in,
And now she takes her loose windbreaker sleeve
To drag the spiny heap over the gravel
And into the weeds, breaking a foxglove
Against its side as if by accident.

I join her to see the black soles of its paws,
Yellow incisors grinning in profile,
Its pale-tipped jaggers aimed from the dead center.
Thrusting dim lights ahead, another car
Drags its pursuing vacuum down the line.
We hold ourselves against the buffeting,
Then walk toward our house and a level bed;
But on the bank she trips out of one sandal
And, sitting down without it, holds her head.

She knows a porcupine is drawn from its life
Or—like the quills shoved out the other side
Of flesh because the irreversible barbs
Take one way out—takes this way out of death.
I rub her foot. No need to mention love.

FILLING OUT A BLANK

High School Profile-Achievement Form for D. Wagoner, 1943 . . . Item 8, Job Preferences: 1) Chemist 2) Stage Magician 3) 1——

My preference was to be
The shrewd man holding up
A test-tube to the light,
Or the bowing charlatan
Whose inexhaustible hat
Could fill a stage with birds.
Lying beyond that,
Nothing seemed like me.

Imagining the years
In a smock or a frock coat
Where all was black or white,
Idly I set about
To conjure up a man
In a glare, concocting life
Like a rich precipitate
By acid out of base.

What shivered up my sleeve
Was neither rabbit nor gold,
But a whole bag of tricks:
The bubbling of retorts
In sterile corridors,
Explosions and handcuffs,
Time falling through trapdoors
In a great cloud of smoke.

But the third guess leaves me cold:
It made me draw a blank,
A stroke drawn with my pen
Going from left to right
And fading out of ink
As casually as a fact.
It came to this brief line,
This disappearing act.

from
STAYING ALIVE
(1966)

THE WORDS

Wind, bird, and tree,
Water, grass, and light:
In half of what I write
Roughly or smoothly
Year by impatient year,
The same six words recur.

I have as many floors
As meadows or rivers,
As much still air as wind
And as many cats in mind
As nests in the branches
To put an end to these.

Instead, I take what is:
The light beats on the stones,
And wind over water shines
Like long grass through the trees,
As I set loose, like birds
In a landscape, the old words.

STAYING ALIVE

Staying alive in the woods is a matter of calming down
At first and deciding whether to wait for rescue,
Trusting to others,
Or simply to start walking and walking in one direction
Till you come out—or something happens to stop you.
By far the safer choice
Is to settle down where you are, and try to make a living
Off the land, camping near water, away from shadows.
Eat no white berries;
Spit out all bitterness. Shooting at anything
Means hiking further and further every day
To hunt survivors;
It may be best to learn what you have to learn without a gun,
Not killing but watching birds and animals go
In and out of shelter
At will. Following their example, build for a whole season:
Facing across the wind in your lean-to,
You may feel wilder,
But nothing, not even you, will have to stay in hiding.
If you have no matches, a stick and a fire-bow
Will keep you warmer,
Or the crystal of your watch, filled with water, held up to
        the sun
Will do the same in time. In case of snow
Drifting toward winter,
Don't try to stay awake through the night, afraid of freezing—
The bottom of your mind knows all about zero;
It will turn you over
And shake you till you waken. If you have trouble sleeping
Even in the best of weather, jumping to follow
With eyes strained to their corners
The unidentifiable noises of the night and feeling
Bears and packs of wolves nuzzling your elbow,
Remember the trappers
Who treated them indifferently and were left alone.
If you hurt yourself, no one will comfort you
Or take your temperature,
So stumbling, wading, and climbing are as dangerous as flying.
But if you decide, at last, you must break through
In spite of all danger,

Think of yourself by time and not by distance, counting
Wherever you're going by how long it takes you;
No other measure
Will bring you safe to nightfall. Follow no streams: they run
Under the ground or fall into wilder country.
Remember the stars
And moss when your mind runs into circles. If it should rain
Or the fog should roll the horizon in around you,
Hold still for hours
Or days if you must, or weeks, for seeing is believing
In the wilderness. And if you find a pathway,
Wheel-rut, or fence-wire,
Retrace it left or right: someone knew where he was going
Once upon a time, and you can follow
Hopefully, somewhere,
Just in case. There may even come, on some uncanny evening,
A time when you're warm and dry, well fed, not thirsty,
Uninjured, without fear,
When nothing, either good or bad, is happening.
This is called staying alive. It's temporary.
What occurs after
Is doubtful. You must always be ready for something to come
    bursting
Through the far edge of a clearing, running toward you,
Grinning from ear to ear
And hoarse with welcome. Or something crossing and
    hovering
Overhead, as light as air, like a break in the sky,
Wondering what you are.
Here you are face to face with the problem of recognition.
Having no time to make smoke, too much to say,
You should have a mirror
With a tiny hole in the back for better aiming, for reflecting
Whatever disaster you can think of, to show
The way you suffer.
These body signals have universal meaning: If you are lying
Flat on your back with arms outstretched behind you,
You say you require
Emergency treatment; if you are standing erect and holding
Arms horizontal, you mean you are not ready;
If you hold them over
Your head, you want to be picked up. Three of anything
Is a sign of distress. Afterward, if you see

No ropes, no ladders,
No maps or messages falling, no searchlights or trails blazing,
Then, chances are, you should be prepared to burrow
Deep for a deep winter.

THE FRUIT OF THE TREE

With a wall and a ditch between us, I watched the gate-legged
    dromedary
Creak open from her sleep and come head-first toward me
As I held out three rust-mottled, tough pears, the color of
    camels.
When I tossed one, she made no move to catch it; whatever
    they eat
Lies still and can wait: the roots and sticks, the scrag-ends of
    brambles.

She straddled, dipping her neck; grey lips and lavender tongue,
Which can choose the best of thorns, thrust the pear to her
    gullet.
Choking, she mouthed it; her ruminating jaw swung up;
Her eyes lashed out. With a groan she crushed it down,
And ecstasy swept her down into the ditch, till her chin

And her pointed, prolonged face sat on the wall. She stared
At me, inventor and founder of pears. I emptied my sack.
She ate them painfully, clumsy with joy, her withers trembling,
Careless of dust on the bitten and dropped halves, ignoring flies,
Losing herself in the pit of her last stomach.

When she gazed at me again, our mouths were both deserted.
I walked away with myself. She watched me disappear,
Then with a rippling trudge went back to her stable
To snort, to browse on hay, to remember my sack forever.
She'd been used to having no pears, but hadn't known it.

Imagine the hostile runners, the biters of burnouses,
Coughers and spitters, whose legs can kick at amazing angles—
Their single humps would carry us willingly over dunes
Through sandstorms and the swirling djinn to the edges of oases
If they, from their waterless, intractable hearts, might stretch
    for pears.

HOUSE-HUNTING

The wind has twisted the roof from an old house
    And thrown it away,
And no one's going to live there anymore.
    It tempts me:
Why not have weather falling in every room?
    Isn't the sky
As easy to keep up as any ceiling?
    Less flat and steady?
Rain is no heavier, soaking heavy heads,
    Than a long party.
Imagine moonlight for a chandelier,
    Sun through the laundry,
The snow on conversation, leaves in the bed,
    Fog in the library,
Or yourself in a bathtub hoping for the best
    As the clouds go by,
Dressing for dinner according to what comes down
    And not how many.
And at night, to sit indoors would be to lose
    Nothing but privacy
As the crossing stars took time to mark their flight
    Over the mind's eye.

THE SHOOTING OF JOHN DILLINGER OUTSIDE THE BIOGRAPH THEATER, JULY 22, 1934

Chicago ran a fever of a hundred and one that groggy Sunday.
A reporter fried an egg on a sidewalk; the air looked shaky.
And a hundred thousand people were in the lake like shirts in
    a laundry.
Why was Johnny lonely?
Not because two dozen solid citizens, heat-struck, had keeled
    over backward.
Not because those lawful souls had fallen out of their sockets
    and melted.
But because the sun went down like a lump in a furnace or a
    bull in the Stockyards.
Where was Johnny headed?
Under the Biograph Theater sign that said, "Our Air is
    Refrigerated."
Past seventeen FBI men and four policemen who stood in
    doorways and sweated.
Johnny sat down in a cold seat to watch Clark Gable get
    electrocuted.
Had Johnny been mistreated?
Yes, but Gable told the D. A. he'd rather fry than be shut up
    forever.
Two women sat by Johnny. One looked sweet, one looked like
    J. Edgar Hoover.
Polly Hamilton made him feel hot, but Anna Sage made him
    shiver.
Was Johnny a good lover?
Yes, but he passed out his share of squeezes and pokes like a
    jittery masher
While Agent Purvis sneaked up and down the aisle like an
    extra usher,
Trying to make sure they wouldn't slip out till the show was
    over.
Was Johnny a fourflusher?
No, not if he knew the game. He got it up or got it back.
But he liked to take snapshots of policemen with his own
    Kodak,
And once in a while he liked to take them with an automatic.
Why was Johnny frantic?

Because he couldn't take a walk or sit down in a movie
Without being afraid he'd run smack into somebody
Who'd point at his rearranged face and holler, "Johnny!"
Was Johnny ugly?
Yes, because Dr. Wilhelm Loeser had given him a new profile
With a baggy jawline and squint eyes and an erased dimple,
With kangaroo-tendon cheekbones and a gigolo's mustache
     that should've been illegal.
Did Johnny love a girl?
Yes, a good-looking, hard-headed Indian named Billie
     Frechette.
He wanted to marry her and lie down and try to get over it,
But she was locked in jail for giving him first-aid and comfort.
Did Johnny feel hurt?
He felt like breaking a bank or jumping over a railing
Into some panicky teller's cage to shout, "Reach for the
     ceiling!"
Or like kicking some vice president in the bum checks and
     smiling.
What was he really doing?
Going up the aisle with the crowd and into the lobby
With Polly saying, "Would *you* do what Clark done?" And
     Johnny saying, "Maybe."
And Anna saying, "If he'd been smart, he'd of acted like Bing
     Crosby."
Did Johnny look flashy?
Yes, his white-on-white shirt and tie were luminous.
His trousers were creased like knives to the tops of his shoes,
And his yellow straw hat came down to his dark glasses.
Was Johnny suspicious?
Yes, and when Agent Purvis signalled with a trembling cigar,
Johnny ducked left and ran out of the theater,
And innocent Polly and squealing Anna were left nowhere.
Was Johnny a fast runner?
No, but he crouched and scurried past a friendly liquor store
Under the coupled arms of double-daters, under awnings,
     under stars,
To the curb at the mouth of an alley. He hunched there.
Was Johnny a thinker?
No, but he was thinking more or less of Billie Frechette
Who was lost in prison for longer than he could possibly wait,
And then it was suddenly too hard to think around a bullet.
Did anyone shoot straight?

Yes, but Mrs. Etta Natalsky fell out from under her picture hat.
Theresa Paulus sprawled on the sidewalk, clutching her left
      foot.
And both of them groaned loud and long under the streetlight.
Did Johnny like that?
No, but he lay down with those strange women, his face in the
      alley,
One shoe off, cinders in his mouth, his eyelids heavy.
When they shouted questions at him, he talked back to
      nobody.
Did Johnny lie easy?
Yes, holding his gun and holding his breath as a last trick,
He waited, but when the Agents came close, his breath
      wouldn't work.
Clark Gable walked his last mile; Johnny ran half a block.
Did he run out of luck?
Yes, before he was cool, they had him spread out on dished-in
      marble
In the Cook County Morgue, surrounded by babbling people
With a crime reporter presiding over the head of the table.
Did Johnny have a soul?
Yes, and it was climbing his slippery wind-pipe like a trapped
      burglar.
It was beating the inside of his ribcage, hollering, "Let me out
      of here!"
Maybe it got out, and maybe it just stayed there.
Was Johnny a money-maker?
Yes, and thousands paid 25¢ to see him, mostly women,
And one said, "I wouldn't have come, except he's a moral
      lesson,"
And another, "I'm disappointed. He feels like a dead man."
Did Johnny have a brain?
Yes, and it always worked best through the worst of dangers,
Through flat-footed hammerlocks, through guarded doors,
      around corners,
But it got taken out in the morgue and sold to some doctors.
Could Johnny take orders?
No, but he stayed in the wicker basket carried by six men
Through the bulging crowd to the hearse and let himself be
      locked in,
And he stayed put as it went driving south in a driving rain.
And he didn't get stolen?
No, not even after his old hard-nosed dad refused to sell

The quick-drawing corpse for $10,000 to somebody in a
    carnival.
He figured he'd let *Johnny* decide how to get to Hell.
Did anyone wish him well?
Yes, half of Indiana camped in the family pasture,
And the minister said, "With luck, he could have been a
    minister."
And up the sleeve of his oversized gray suit, Johnny twitched
    a finger.
Does anyone remember?
Everyone still alive. And some dead ones. It was a new kind of
    holiday
With hot and cold drinks and hot and cold tears. They planted
    him in a cemetery
With three unknown vice presidents, Benjamin Harrison, and
    James Whitcomb Riley,
Who never held up anybody.

THE DRAFTSMEN, 1945

Given one wall and a roof at a wild angle,
The problem was to find the rest of the house
In Engineering Drawing, to string it along
Its three spread-eagled ninety-degree dimensions
 (A line is only a line when it lies flat) ,
Then trace it up and over, tracking it down
At last to a blunt façade with a shut door.

The whole hot room of us on dunces' stools
Maneuvered compasses and triangles
Over the sliding T-squares and onion skin,
Trying to be on all six sides of a house
At the same time, locking slabs in place
As firmly as the edges of our graves.

We stared at the box like catty-cornered neighbors
Or, losing our perspective, swivelled the earth
Like one-eyed gods till porches spread their wings
And the slant sunlight's isometric waves
Levelled all distance, simply, at a stroke.

And that was that—top, profiles, and front view,
The backside and the rat's collapsible heaven:
Spaces cut out of space like paper dolls
And modelled on a blank interior.

None of us had to draw it inside out,
Sketch in the beds, let smoke through broken windows,
Locate the milkman bleeding in the garden,

Or cross-hatch people running off the paper
Where weather crumpled the uneven corners,

Or knock at the door for any other answers.

THE NIGHT OF THE SAD WOMEN

They are undressing slowly by closed doors,
Unable to find themselves, fading in mirrors
And feeling faint, finding their eyes in time
But seeing, instead, the rooms behind their shoulders

Where nothing is going to work, where photographs
Stand still in frames, arresting other days
When things were turning out. Now turning in,
They are lowering shades and turning off the lights,

But find their fingers lighter than pale linen
At the sinking bedside, seeing their own hands
In front of their faces wavering like gauze,
Then edging away to search in fallen purses.

But they lose touch. In the middle of their rooms
The night begins, the night of the loose threads
Which hang like spiders' lifelines out of seams
To be ravelled to the floor, but not to end.

WATER MUSIC FOR THE PROGRESS
OF LOVE IN A LIFE-RAFT
DOWN THE SAMMAMISH SLOUGH

Slipping at long last from the shore, we wave
        To no one in a house
With a dismantled chimney, a sprung gate,
        And five bare windows,
And begin this excursion under thorny vines
        Trailing like streamers
Over the mainstream, in our inflated life-raft,
        Bluer and yellower
Than the sky and sun which hold the day together.
        My love, upstream,
Be the eyes behind me, saying yes and no.
        I'm manning the short oars
Which must carry us with the current, or without it,
        Six miles to our pasture.
There go the mallards patched with grey and white
        By their tame fathers;
Down from the leaves the kingfishers branching go
        Raucous under the willows
And out of sight; the star-backed salmon are waiting
        For the rain to rise above us;
And the wind is sending our raft like a water spider
        Skimming over the surface.
We begin our lesson here, our slight slow progress,
        Sitting face to face,
Able to touch our hands or soaking feet
        But not to kiss
As long as we must wait at opposite ends,
        Keeping our balance,
Our spirits cold as the Sammamish mud,
        Our tempers rising
Among the drifts like the last of the rainbows rising
        Through the remaining hours
Till the sun goes out. What have I done to us?
        I offer these strands,
These unromantic strains, unable to give
        Such royal accompaniment
As horns on the Thames or bronze bells on the Nile
        Or the pipes of goatmen,

But here, the goats themselves in the dying reeds,
        The ringing cows
And bullocks on the banks, pausing to stare
        At our confluence
Along the awkward passage to the bridge
        Over love's divisions.
Landing at nightfall, letting the air run out
        Of what constrained us,
We fold it together, crossing stem to stern,
        Search for our eyes,
And reach ourselves, in time, to wake again
        This music from silence.

THE POETS AGREE TO BE QUIET
BY THE SWAMP

They hold their hands over their mouths
And stare at the stretch of water.
What can be said has been said before:
Strokes of light like herons' legs in the cattails,
Mud underneath, frogs lying even deeper.
Therefore, the poets may keep quiet.
But the corners of their mouths grin past their hands.
They stick their elbows out into the evening,
Stoop, and begin the ancient croaking.

THE MAN OF THE HOUSE

My father, looking for trouble, would find it
On his hands and knees by hammering on walls
Between the joists or drilling through baseboards
Or crawling into the attic where insulation
Lay under the leaks like sleeping-bags.

It would be something simple as a rule
To be ingenious for, in overalls;
And he would kneel beside it, pouring sweat
Down his red cheeks, glad of a useful day
With something wrong unknown to the landlord.

At those odd times when everything seemed to work
All right, suspiciously all right like silence
In concrete shelters, he'd test whatever hung
Over our heads: such afternoons meant ladders,
Nails in the mouth, flashing and shaking roofs.

In safety shoes going down basement stairs,
He'd flick his rewired rearrangement of lights
And chase all shadows into the coalbin
Where they could watch him, blinking at his glare.
If shadows hadn't worked, he would have made them.

With hands turning to horn against the stone
He'd think on all fours, hunch as if to drink
If his cold chisel broke the cold foundation
And brought dark water pulsing out of clay.
Wrenching at rows of pipes like his cage-bars,

He made them creak in sockets and give way,
But rammed them back, putting his house in order.
Moonlight or rain, after the evening paper,
His mouth lay open under the perfect plaster
To catch the first sweet drop, but none came down.

FOR THE WARMING
OF AN ARTIST'S STUDIO

The previous tenant, running out of business,
Bolted the back door,
Blew out the fuses, sprang the toilet trap,
Unscrewed the hardware,
And didn't leave a trace of his side-kicks—
No cold cashier
Behind the hole in the window saying No,
And no go-getter
Coughing to break the gathering punch-line
At the water-cooler.
Tonight, we'll drink to him. He left the ceiling,
The best part of the floor,
And enough strength in the walls to take the weight
Of an easel's crossbar
On which to float some stock in an enterprise
Also going under
Eventually after going upside-down,
Slantwise and haywire,
But never simply crossing into the red
Like a line in a ledger.
Here goes an artist after a businessman
Not as a panhandler
But, following him through rundown neighborhoods
And making over
The empty premises at the end of his line,
As a silent partner.

WAITING ON THE CURB

Death: "Everyman, stand still."

Stalled by the traffic, waiting for the light
And giving a little at the knees, I stand
As still at others tied up in their shoes.
Looking ahead, my eyes switch out of sight,
Commemorating death by doing nothing
And needing a signal to get over it.

Behind my packages, I sweat it out,
Having already memorized the corner—
The fireplug, street-sign, waste-can, cracked cement
With which our city civilizes dirt—
And, feeling cornered, shuffle to keep warm,
Knowing it's useless now to plant my feet.

Ahead of me, all out from under arrest
And rushing suddenly over the jammed street,
The others hurry off to make up time;
But losing this moment, Death, I wait for you
To let me go. My disobedient body
Clings to my spine like a drunk to a lamppost.

NIGHT PASSAGE

The lights are going on over the water.
Over the ridge of the disappearing island
Headlights rise and fall like the ledge of the sun,
And starlight shiftier than eyes
Across the headland flashes the end of day.

Out of the houses and the fading woods,
On the water (scarlet
For rocks and the glimmering starboard landfall)
From the depths, the burning creatures come,
Their luminous slow heads touching the night.

Lights coming on in the dark look out of holes
At others burnt to sleep in the distance,
My mind, going out among them, going out.

BY THE ORCHARD

Rushing through leaves, they fall
Down, abruptly down
To the ground, bumping the branches,
The windfall apples falling
Yellow into the long grass and lying
Where they have fallen
In the tree's shadow, the shades
Of their soft bruises sinking, opening wide
Mouths to the mouths of creatures
Who like the sun are falling
To flicker, to worm's end under
Themselves, the hatch of moons.

GOING TO PIECES

Pull yourself together, pal.
—advice from a stranger

Those marionette-show skeletons can do it
Suddenly, after their skulls have been
Alone in the rafters, after their wishbones
Have fluttered in the wings, leaving the feet onstage
To hoof it solo: they pull themselves together,
Bring everything back and thread it on their spines.

But looking around and seeing other people
Coming apart at parties, breaking up
And catching their own laughter in both hands,
Or crossing the lawn and throwing up their spirits
Like voice-balloons in funnies, touching noses
In bedroom mirrors, one after another,
I figure something can be said for it:
Maybe some people break in better halves
Or some of the parts are greater than the whole.

Pal, take a look around: a heap of coats
Discarded in one spot like empty skins;
Under the tables enough shoes and gloves,
Enough loose hair, saliva, and fingernails
To conjure bodies off a hundred souls.
Now I'll tell you one: the palolo worms,
One night a year at the bottom of the sea,
Back halfway out of the burrows where they spend
Long lives; their tails turn luminous, twist free,
And all by themselves swim up to the surface,
Joining with millions of other detached tails;
The sea in a writhing mass lies white for miles
Under a gibbous moon; the bright halves die
And float away like scraps after a party,
But leave behind their larvae, set for life.

Meanwhile, the old ones, steady in their holes
Can go about their business, fanning food
Into their sleek, uninterrupted gullets.
Think of them there, pal, chewing the ocean,
Staying alive by going to pieces.

STRETCHING CANVASES

By the last of the light, I pull
Over firm stretcher-bars
The ends of the last canvas
You wanted, miter the corners
Like sheets on a guest-bed,
And staple them on tight.
Stark white, three in a row
Are leaning on our house
To catch at the sunset.
From their surfaces, the stream
Of the undivided spectrum—
The whole palette of light—
Has put out both my eyes.
Good luck, my darling.
I can't see a thing.
My hammer flustered crows
All afternoon, kept jays
Out of the hazel trees.
I'm an aimless carpenter,
And now it's going to be winter
By the rule of this blue thumb.
We need storm-windows
In frames exactly like these.
Good luck to the canvas
Under the boxer's back
And the sail over the circus;
And good luck, facing you,
To the three against the wall
Which may be windows yet.
Keeping the storms in mind
And brushing the sky light
Like the stubble of the wind,
Look through, darling, look through.

THE WELCOME

For leagues the bunting rose on telephone wires,
And we made way like gates, giving away
Everything handy, gingering old horses
And pressing back as plastered as posters
Against the shop-fronts, spilling their bargains.
Balloons blew wholesale out of the mouths of tubas,
Billboards collapsed on multicolored hams,
And we waited. His lunch lay thawed in restaurants,
His cushions plumped, the girls asleep in cakes,
The corks already popped out of his magnums.
Our faces, all one way, went on and off
Like blinkers down the deserted lanes of the street.
Slowly the peach and lavender gulls stopped flying.

And he arrived on the wrong side of town
With no doors sighing open, no rushing lipstick,
And no quick squeezes for the quick or the dead.
Jaywalking over rails and safety-islands,
Through lawns and alleys, bumping barbecues
And shuffling straight through hedges and ash piles,
Trespassing yards with dogs dogging his heels,
Through summer mulch, the vee's of broken clotheslines
Following him like geese over our fences,
He slipped into the vacant heart of the city
And out the other side without a word.

REVIVAL

for Richard Hugo

When Brother Jessen showed the tawny spot
On the carpet where a man threw up a demon,
He had another man by the ear
Beside the rose-covered plastic cross. He shouted
Into that ear a dozen times in a row,
"I curse you, Demon, in the name of Jesus!"
Some of his flock clapped hands. He knelt and sweated.
"They can try skating and wienie roasts," he said,
"But that don't keep the kids out of lovers' lane."
He pointed at me. "You don't believe in demons."

Next door, they were chasing some with double shots,
And the wind was up, and it was one of those nights
When it's hard to breathe
And you can't sit or talk, when your eyes focus
On all disjointed scraps shoved into corners,
And something's going to happen. People feel fine,
Brother Jessen says, if they can lose their demons.
They wash in showers of everlasting dew
Which is the sweat of angels sick for men.

The demon has names, he told me, like Rebellion,
And it won't submit, it wants a cup of coffee,
Wants to go for a walk, and like as not
Turns up in Hell. Hugo, if you and I,
Having been cursed by some tough guy like Jesus,
Were to lose that wild, squat, bloody, grinning demon
Locked in the pit of our respective guts,
Whose fork has pitched us, flattened us to walls,
Left us in alleys where the moon smells dead,
Or jerked us out of the arms of our wives to write
Something like this, we'd sprawl flat on the floor,
A couple of tame spots at a revival.

Let's save a little sweat for the bad guys
Who can't keep out of lovers' lane for a minute,
Who, when they trip, will lie there in the rut
For old time's sake, rebellious as all Hell,
Croaking forever, loving the hard way.

76

TALKING TO THE FOREST

"When we can understand animals, we will know the change is halfway. When we can talk to the forest, we will know that the change has come."
—Andrew Joe, Skagit Tribe, Washington

We'll notice first they've quit turning their ears
To catch our voices drifting through cage-bars,
The whites of their eyes no longer shining from corners.
And all dumb animals suddenly struck dumb
Will turn away, embarrassed by a change
Among our hoots and catcalls, whistles and snorts
That crowd the air as tightly as ground-mist.

The cassowary pacing the hurricane fence,
The owl on the driftwood, the gorilla with folding arms,
The buffalo aimed all day in one direction,
The bear on his rock—will need no talking to,
Spending their time so deeply wrapped in time
(Where words lie down like the lion and the lamb)
Not even their own language could reach them.

And so, we'll have to get out of the zoo
To the forest, rain or shine, whichever comes
Dropping its downright shafts before our eyes,
And think of something to say, using new words
That won't turn back bewildered, lost or scattered
Or panicked, curling under the first bush
To wait for a loud voice to hunt them out,

Not words that fall from the skin looking like water
And running together, meaning anything,
Then disappearing into the forest floor
Through gray-green moss and ferns rotting in shade,
Not words like crown-fire overhead, but words
Like old trees felled by themselves in the wilderness,
Making no noise unless someone is listening.

WALKING IN THE SNOW

". . . if the author had said, 'Let us put on appropriate
galoshes,' there could, of course, have been no poem . . ."
—an analysis of Elinor Wylie's "Velvet Shoes,"
College English, March 1948, p. 319.

Let us put on appropriate galoshes, letting them flap open,
And walk in the snow.
The eyes have fallen out of the nearest snowman;
It slumps in its shadow,
And the slush at the curb is gray as the breasts of gulls.
As we slog together
Past arbors and stiff trees, all knocked out cold
At the broken end of winter,
No matter what may be falling out of the sky
Or blowing sideways
Against our hearts, we'll make up our own weather.
Love, stamping our galoshes,
Let's say something inappropriate, something flat
As a scholar's ear
And, since this can't be a poem, something loud
And pointless, leading nowhere
Like our footprints ducking and draking in the snow
One after the other.

AN AFTERNOON ON THE GROUND

The ducks and the green drakes
Covered flooded fields.
The herons struck themselves
Aslant in the flowing moss,
And pinetrees, burnt with crows,
Stood short of the mountains.
One hawk rose through the sun,
Casting no shadow down.

These thoughts were five miles long,
Stretched on a river road
Over a frail bridge
Past swampland and meadow
To the prison's honor farm
Where, ghost-pale to the waist,
Running in bare feet,
The trusties were playing ball.

How could I hold them all
Between the sides of my head?
The ducks were as good as gone,
The river would calm down,
The frogs and herons would fly
Together or separately
Like water through the air
Or air over the water,
And the crows all scatter
And the mountain behind them
Be a mountain in a poem
Off which nothing could fall,
And the hawk turn into feathers.

Along that stretch of river
For five miles, hanging on
To the truth of the matter
That led from birds to men,
I had trailed it after me.
But suddenly it tightened.
The end slipped out of my mind,
And the bare-backed prisoners
Were running around a field
On the first good day of spring,
Lifting their arms and shouting.

SLEEPING BY A RIVER

My feet cut off from me, the ends of my legs
As heavy as the stones they're lying on,
One hand cupped empty over my forehead,
I wake by the riverside, catching myself
Napping, open-mouthed under a cloud.

A rock stuck in my back like a revolver
Holds me up a moment, lets me down
To this numb heap of matter
Whose pieces won't rouse out. I should have known
Better than this. There isn't one dumb creature

Back in the woods who'd fall asleep out here.
There's too much give and take out in the open.
Someone moved the sun when I wasn't looking
And did me to a turn as red as leaves.
Here come the flies across the hatch of evening.

And something drank my spirits while I slept,
Then corked me like a bottle without a message.
It coaxed the soul out of my fingertips,
Spun out its prints as vaguely as whirlpools,
Rippled across my forehead, and flew off.

I shift my upper eye to see the crows
Leaving an alder, full of their dark selves.
This is the way it goes.
The soul goes straight away as the crow flies
With enough noise to wake what's left behind
And leave it, one eye up, like a dying salmon.

AFTER FALLING

Sleep lightly, sleep eventfully
That from the jangling backs of your eyes may come the
    harness
Without horses, the trappings of darkness
And a country in pieces wedged across pale hills
And out of the mind—through fields ragged with light
Where the wrong birds out of season
Crouch in the grass, their wings trembling like eyelids.

Sleep watchfully, now, leaning across
The long strands holding the night like reins through
    clouds
And darkening with them, flourishing into water
Where the rough road divides repeatedly,
Dissolving slowly, streaming over the ground
But springing again, as the birds will,
To climb through wilder country before falling.

A VALEDICTORY TO
STANDARD OIL OF INDIANA

In the darkness east of Chicago, the sky burns over the
    plumbers' nightmares
Red and blue, and my hometown lies there loaded with
    gasoline.
Registers ring like gas-pumps, pumps like pinballs, pinballs like
    broken alarm clocks,
And it's time for morning, but nothing's going to work.
From cat-cracker to candle-shop, from grease-works along the
    pipeline,
Over storage tanks like kings on a checkerboard ready to jump
    the county,
The word goes out: With refined regrets
We suggest you sleep all day in your houses shaped like lunch
    buckets
And don't show up at the automated gates.
Something else will tap the gauges without yawning
And check the valves at the feet of the cooling-towers without
    complaining.
Standard Oil is canning my high school classmates
And the ones who fell out of junior high or slipped in the grades.
What should they do, gassed up in their Tempests and Comets,
    raring to go
Somewhere with their wives scowling in front and kids stuffed
    in the back,
Past drive-ins jammed like car-lots, trying to find the beaches
But blocked by freights for hours, stopped dead in their tracks
Where the rails, as thick as thieves along the lakefront,
Lower their crossing gates to shut the frontier? What can they
    think about
As they stare at the sides of boxcars for a sign,
And Lake Michigan drains slowly into Lake Huron,
The mills level the Dunes, and the eels go sailing through the
    trout,
And mosquitoes inherit the evening, while toads no bigger than
    horseflies
Hop crazily after them over the lawns and sidewalks, and the
    rainbows fall
Flat in the oil they came from? There are two towns now,
One dark, one going to be dark, divided by cyclone fences:

One pampered and cared for like pillboxes and cathedrals,
The other vanishing overnight in the dumps and swamps like a
    struck sideshow.
As the Laureate of the Class of '44—which doesn't know it has
    one—
I offer this poem, not from hustings or barricades
Or the rickety stage where George Rogers Clark stood glued to
    the wall,
But from another way out, like Barnum's "This Way to the
    Egress,"
Which moved the suckers when they'd seen enough. Get out of
    town.

THE CIRCUIT

My circuit-riding great-grandfather
Rode off on horseback through the hickory woods
Each week to galvanize five Methodist churches,
And once, passing a Sabbath-breaking auction,
Shouted over his shoulder, "Fifteen cents!"
They caught him miles away
And saddled him with an old grandfather clock.

What got you up on your horse in the morning, sir?
Did you rehearse damnation
Till the trees fell crossways like a corduroy road?
Did anyone catch his death, as you caught yours,
Coming to hear you freezing in a shed?
Nobody mentions anything you did
Except the clock—no name-dropping of God,
No chiming adage. A joke thrown back of a horse
Has lasted longer than your rules and reasons.

I saw you stiff as a tintype in your bed
Next to a basin and a worn-out Bible,
Your beard aimed at the ceiling like a sermon.
Over the distance I can hear you shouting,
"Where in the name of God is the Name of God
In all these damned unsingable useless poems?"

Your family fought harder for the clock
Than they did for souls, and now they know its face
Better than yours, having replaced the works.
Beards are no longer hanging out of pulpits;
If God speaks from a bush, it's only by chance.
I shave my face and wait,
But bid for every clock I lay my eyes on
Just for the hell of it, your Hell and mine.
Like you, I'm doing time in the hard woods,
Tracking myself in circles, a lost preacher.

SPEECH FROM A COMEDY

Scene: The wreckage of Heaven

I am God. But all my creatures are unkind to me.
They think of themselves. Why don't they think of me?
I'm holier than they.
   Chorus God is lovely.
If I descended and rode through the streets,
Would they take off their hats?
No, they'd keep their hands in each other's pockets.
   Chorus God is out of sorts.
Or if I showed up to give a formal address
Including an enormous amount of sound, godly advice,
They'd turn and wriggle away like a school of fish.
   Chorus God is endless.
I burned myself in a bush once. Day and night,
I burned like a pillar of virtue in the desert.
I even let them watch me ride in my chariot.
   Chorus God is great.
I gave them Aaron's rod when they were on the rocks.
I plagued their enemies with a thousand dirty tricks.
I let them burn rams in thickets instead of their precious
  Isaacs.
   Chorus God is on their backs.
When things looked so black they couldn't tell his from
  hers,
I parted the waters,
Saving a few. But drowning a lot of others.
   Chorus God is feeling worse.
Didn't I die for them?
Hang myself? And shed the Blood of the Lamb?
What more could I do? Try it yourself sometime.
   Chorus God is sublime.
Now they forsake me. Leave me up in the air.
Sinning. Thinking of pleasure.
The more I leave them alone, the worse they are.
   Chorus God is pure.
They lie all night in their houses stacked in rows,
Their knees pulled up, their heads stuffed into pillows,
Imagining new ways to break my laws.
   Chorus God is jealous.

85

When I show them a bad example, plastered and confused,
Chances are he'll be headlined and idolized.
The only law of mine they like is getting circumcised.
       Chorus   God is not amused.
I didn't ask for anything impossible.
I said, "Love me—and not just once in a while."
But all men were created fickle.
       Chorus   God is immortal.
I'll settle with Everyman.
I had his dinner all laid out in my mansion,
But *he* had to try cooking his *own*.
       Chorus   God is burning.
Just because angels are blasé and neuter,
Did he think I'd be contented forever and ever
Playing with Ezekiel's wheel or climbing up and down
    Jacob's ladder?
       Chorus   God is boiling over.
I made him in my image, didn't I?
I gave him my tooth for a tooth, my eye for an eye.
How could I turn out such an unreasonable facsimile?
       Chorus   God is mighty sorry.
He'll be made to see the way things really are.
If he's so fond of slaughter,
I can get it for him wholesale just by losing my temper.
       Chorus   God's a man-of-war.
I might have shown him mercy,
But nobody asked me.
The best things in Heaven are costly.
       Chorus   God is free.
All right, he's dug his bed. Now let him lie in it
A thousand years at a stretch on a strict diet
While worms with their noses on fire pay an endless visit.
       Chorus   God is like that.
I watched over him like a shepherd over a sheep
While he went bleating and gambolling and flocking
    around and getting fleeced, forgetting whom to
    worship.
Well, every shepherd knows his way to the butchershop.
       Chorus   God is in bad shape.
Come, Death. He has made me mad.
I summon Death. For his ingratitude,
Everyman must choke on his daily bread.
       Chorus   God is sick and tired.

THE OSPREY'S NEST

The osprey's nest has dropped of its own weight
After years, breaking everything under it, collapsing
Out of the sky like the wreckage of the moon,
Having killed its branch and rotted its lodgepole:
A flying cloud of fishbones tall as a man,
A shambles of dead storms ten feet across.

Uncertain what holds anything together,
Ospreys try everything—fishnets and broomsticks,
Welcome-mats and pieces of scarecrows,
Sheep bones, shells, the folded wings of mallards—
And heap up generations till they topple.

In the nest the young ones, calling fish to fly
Over the water toward them in old talons,
Thought only of hunger diving down their throats
To the heart, not letting go— (not letting go,
Ospreys have washed ashore, ruffled and calm
But drowned, their claws embedded in salmon).
They saw the world was bones and curtain-rods,
Hay-wire and cornstalks—rubble put to bed
And glued into meaning by large appetites.
Living on top of everything that mattered,
The fledglings held it in the air with their eyes,
With awkward claws groping the ghosts of fish.

Last night they slapped themselves into the wind
And cried across the rain, flopping for comfort
Against the nearest branches, baffled by leaves
And the blank darkness falling below their breasts.
Where have they gone? The nest, now heaped on the
        bank,
Has come to earth smelling as high as heaven.

MAKING UP FOR A SOUL

It's been like fixing a clock, jamming the wheels,
The pinions, and bent springs into a box
And shaking it. Or like patching a vase,
Gluing the mismatched edges of events
Together despite the quirks in the design.
Or trying to make one out of scraps of paper,
The yellowing, dog-eared pages going slapdash
Over each other, flat as a collage.
I can't keep time with it. It won't hold water.
Ripping and rearranging make no pattern.

Imagine me with a soul: I'm sitting here
In the room with you, smiling from corner to corner,
My chest going up and down with inspiration.
I sit serene, insufferably at my ease,
Not scratching or drumming but merely suffering
Your questions, like the man from the back of the book
With all the answers. You couldn't stand me, could you?

My love, if *you* have a soul, don't tell me yet.
Why can't we simply stay uneasy together?
There are snap-on souls like luminous neckties
That light up in the dark, spelling our names.
Let's put them on for solemn visitors,
Switch off the lights, then grope from room to room,
Making our hollow, diabolical noises
Like Dracula and his spouse, avoiding mirrors,
Clutching each other fiendishly for life
To stop the gaps in ourselves, like better halves.

OBSERVATIONS FROM THE OUTER EDGE

I pass the abrupt end of the woods, and stop.
I'm standing on a cliff as sheer as a step
Where the ground, like the ground floor of a nightmare,
Has slipped a notch six hundred rocky feet
And left itself in the lurch. My shoes go dead.
Not looking yet, I let my heart sneak back,

But feel like the fall-guy ending a Western,
The heavy, bound to topple from the edge
And disappear with terrible gravity.
I put my hand out in the separate air
With nothing under it, but it feels nothing.
This is no place for putting my foot down,

So I shout my name, but can't scare up an echo.
No one inside this canyon wants to be me.
I manage to look down. Not much to envy:
The silent, immobile rapids, the toy pines,
A fisherman stuck in the shallows like an agate—
A world so far away, it could quit moving

And I wouldn't know the difference. I've seen it before
At the ends of hallways, the far sides of windows,
Shrinking from sight. Down is no worse than across.
Whether it's sky, horizon, or ground zero,
A piece of space will take whatever comes
From any direction—climbing, walking, or falling.

I remember a newsreel—a man holding a baby
Over the Grand Canyon on a stick:
The kid hung on and grinned for the camera.
I grab the nearest branch just to make sure
It isn't death down there, looking like hell.
Even a mountain goat will go to pieces

Standing on glass suspended in the air,
But man created with a jerkier balance
Can learn to fix his eyes on a safe place.
Trembling somewhere,
The acrophobiac Primum Mobile
Clings to his starry axle, staring sideways.

LEAVING SOMETHING BEHIND

A fox at your neck and snakeskin on your feet,
You have gone to the city behind an ivory brooch,
Wearing your charms for and against desire, bearing your
    beauty
Past all the gaping doorways, amazing women on edge
And leading men's eyes astray while skirting mayhem,
And I, for a day, must wish you safe in your skin.

The diggers named her the Minnesota Girl. She was fifteen,
Eight thousand years ago, when she drowned in a glacial
    lake,
Curling to sleep like her sea-snail amulet, holding a
    turtleshell,
A wolf's tooth, the tine of an antler, carrying somehow
A dozen bones from the feet of water birds. She believed
    in her charms,
But something found her and kept her. She became what
    she wore.

She loved her bones and her own husk of creatures
But left them piecemeal on the branching shore.
Without you, fox paws, elephant haunches, all rattling tails,
Snails' feet, turtles' remote hearts, muzzles of wolves,
Stags' ears, and the tongues of water birds are only
    themselves.
Come safely back. There was nothing in her arms.

WORKING AGAINST TIME

By the newly bulldozed logging road, for a hundred yards,
I saw the sprawling five-foot hemlocks, their branches
      crammed
Into each other's light, upended or wrenched aslant
Or broken across waists the size of broomsticks
Or bent, crushed slewfoot on themselves in the duff like
      briars,
Their roots coming at random out of the dirt, and dying.

I had no burlap in the trunk, not even a spade,
And the shirt off my back wasn't enough to go around.
I'm no tree surgeon, it wasn't Arbor Day, but I climbed
Over the free-for-all, untangling winners and losers
And squeezing as many as I could into my car.
When I started, nothing was singing in the woods except me.

I hardly had room to steer—roots dangled over my shoulder
And scraped the side of my throat as if looking for water.
Branches against the fog on the windshield dabbled designs
Like kids or hung out the vent. The sun was falling down.
It's against the law to dig up trees. Working against
Time and across laws, I drove my ambulance

Forty miles in the dark to the house and began digging
Knee-deep graves for most of them, while the splayed
      headlights
Along the highway picked me out of the night:
A fool with a shovel searching for worms or treasure,
Both buried behind the sweat on his forehead. Two green
      survivors
Are tangled under the biting rain as I say this.

A ROOM WITH A VIEW

1

At last, outside my window an expanse
For the mind's elbows, stretching north and south:
Houseboats and towers, drydocks and seaplanes,
Streets vaulting over hillsides
And the top of the sky pushed backward through the
    clouds,
Then over high bridges into the distance
Where the sun is breaking, falling beyond the mountains.

In the darkness, blazing like campfires locked in glass,
The lights from other houses
Survive the invisible weather of the night.
I watch through the dawn
Cars butting each other down long chutes to the city
And the black-decked seiner circling the inlet,
Dragging its purse behind, then slewing away
With the morning offering, leaving the water empty.

2

Looking up from a book or half a sentence
For some way out, I've seen from other rooms
Weeds sloping up to brambles, telephone wires,
Or strips of grass like runners between neighbors,
Or only the sweating windows
Themselves, as blank as paper, or streaky shades
Like moths too big and battered to get out.

Now the reach and stretch of this astounding air
Unfocuses my eyes. Whatever is coming
Must come from as far away as the horizon.
To see what I could only imagine once
When, shut in a box, I heard hard winter knocking,
Makes me afraid. Having set myself to think,

Having arranged to watch the weather coming,
I'm afraid it won't be real:
The wind in a single lane, the clouds in rows,
The lightning mastered in an orderly sheaf,
The snow and sleet in clusters,
The uniform thunder rolling itself flat.

A man in a room with a view draws back—
As though on a cliff—from the edge of the operatic,
Tempted to own it, to get above himself.
Poets and *helden* tenors, straining for height,
Mistake the roaring in their ears for the ocean.

3
In a small glass box I've made a terrarium:
Eight kinds of moss from the banks of mountain streams
Whose interlacing fern-like leaves
And outflung sporophytes like spears in a mob-scene
Make perfect sense from only a foot away,
As unpredictably various as a shrine
In a Zen garden, or a piece of forest floor
Where every inch of the dead is crammed with blossoms.

If I grew tired as a god and forgot its water
Or dumped it out the window
Or set out scientifically to destroy it
By fire or drowning or some kind of mayhem,
The least fragment, a half-burnt speck or spore
Or the most unlikely single rootless cell,
Where the green goes dark as night, could breed again
An entire garden. Here, pressed against the glass
On four high sides like the corners of the world,
It breathes my breath. Its weather is my face.

COME BEFORE HIS COUNTENANCE
WITH A JOYFUL LEAPING

Swivelling flat-soled on the dirt but ready to bound in arches
    at the nick of time, spurring yourselves, come all as
    you are with footbones rattling like claques, with
    storking knees careering into the crooked distance,
    horning in and out of sight,
Come coasting in circles, rearing, running aground, and
    flickering up the air, peeling and flaking away like
    handbills over the sloping daylight,
Come lambing and fishing, outflanking the body's heights at a
    single stroke, out of breath, out at the elbows,
    spreading blank palms and flinching up hillsides
    hoisted out of mind,
Come at a loss out of manholes and sandtraps, jerking free at
    the heart, assaulted and blinking on dislocated ankles,
    swollen with song from the twisted wreckage, dying
    and rigorous after the second wind,
For He is falling apart in His unstrung parbuckles, His beard
    blown loose by harmonious unction, His countenance
    breaking, His fragments flopping up and around
    without us to the stretches of morning.

SONG TO ACCOMPANY
THE BEARER OF BAD NEWS

Kings kill their messengers
Sometimes, slicing wildly
Through pages delivering their grief
And you may do the same
With this page under this poem
Tear it lengthwise first
With feeling, cutting off
Each phrase into meaningless halves
Then crossways, severing
The mild beginning from the bad ending
By now you know the worst
Having imagined the remainder
Down to the painful inch
Where something like your name
Closes this message
You needn't finish now
You may stop here
And puzzle it out later.

Kings kill
Sometimes, slicing
Through pages
And you may
With this page
Tear it
With feeling
Each phrase
Then crossways
The mild beginning
By now you know
Having imagined
Down to
Where something
Closes
You needn't finish
You may stop
And puzzle it out.

Their messengers
Wildly

Delivering their grief
Do the same
Under this poem
Lengthwise first
Cutting off
Into meaningless halves
Severing
The bad ending
The worst
The remainder
The painful inch
Like your name
This message
Now
Here
Later

You may   tear it   into meaningless halves
Lengthwise first   then crossways
Severing   something like   the painful inch
Later   under this poem   messengers
Delivering their grief   puzzle it out
Having imagined   the worst
Kings kill   wildly   through pages
Cutting off   the bad ending
Do the same   with this page
By now you know   the mild beginning
Down to where   your name   closes
With feeling   now   you may stop.

from
NEW AND SELECTED POEMS
(1969)

AT ST. VINCENT DEPAUL'S

"Free shoes, help yourself"

Buckling their thin soles,
These squads of shoes
In lines under the rain
Are shining this morning,
Rocking on round heels
Or turning up at the toes
As if to jump for joy
Or jump out of the way:
Oxfords and safety shoes
And boots whose arches fell
Flatter than handprints
Are warping back to life,
The cracked and wrinkled hides
As supple as fishskins
Now in the falling water
Under their own steam
Like the rising ghosts of socks,
The sneakers stuck together,
Slippers whose pompons
Bloom like anemones,
Golf shoes for trespassing,
The tongueless, the mismatched
For an hour helping themselves,
Free as long as they last.

BUMS AT BREAKFAST

Daily, the bums sat down to eat in our kitchen.
They seemed to be whatever the day was like:
If it was hot or cold, they were hot or cold;
If it was wet, they came in dripping wet.
One left his snowy shoes on the back porch
But his socks stuck to the clean linoleum,
And one, when my mother led him to the sink,
Wrung out his hat instead of washing his hands.

My father said they'd made a mark on the house,
A hobo's sign on the sidewalk, pointing the way.
I hunted everywhere, but never found it.
It must have said, "It's only good in the morning—
When the husband's out." My father knew by heart
Lectures on Thrift and Doggedness,
But he was always either working or sleeping.
My mother didn't know any advice.

They ate their food politely, with old hands,
Not looking around, and spoke in short, plain answers.
Sometimes they said what they'd been doing lately
Or told us what was wrong; but listening hard,
I broke their language into secret codes:
Their *east* meant *west,* their *job* meant *walking and
        walking,*
Their *money* meant *danger, home* meant *running and
        hiding,*
Their *father* and *mother* were different kinds of weather.

Dumbly, I watched them leave by the back door,
Their pockets empty as a ten-year-old's;
Yet they looked twice as rich, being full of breakfast.
I carried mine like a lump all the way to school.
When I was growing hungry, where would they be?
None ever came twice. Never to lunch or dinner.
They were always starting fresh in the fresh morning.
I dreamed of days that stopped at the beginning.

BLUES TO BE SUNG IN A DARK VOICE

It's time to shine the bottom of my shoes.
Move over, cousin. Here comes my bad news.
Goodbye, good boy. Hello, hello, blues.
>   *spoken*   Milkman won't milk me, tailor won't
>   suit me now.
So goodbye, good boy.

Florist won't let me smell his kind of bunch.
Grocer won't deliver me, that's a cinch.
Banker won't check me out to drink some lunch.
>   *spoken*   Jeweler just watches, he don't ring
>   me up.
So goodbye, good boy.

Dealer won't cut me in on his old game.
Sheriff don't teach me how to spell my name.
Driver won't bus me, I'll get there just the same.
>   *spoken*   Garbageman don't give me no
>   pick-me-ups.
So goodbye, good boy.

Shoe-man won't put bottoms on my tops.
Druggist drug me down to see the cops.
Plumber won't bail me out, I'm here for keeps.
>   *spoken*   Railroads won't forgive my
>   trespasses.
So goodbye, good boy.

Baker ain't going to roll me any more.
Barber ain't going to clip me like before.
Mama can't get my knees down on the floor.
>   *spoken*   Doctor won't take my pulse 'cause he
>   can't keep it.
So goodbye, good boy.

Loan-man likes that X on the dotted line.
Preacher, he keeps crossing me all the time:
Someone sets fire to it, it burns just fine.
>   *spoken*   Landlord ain't going to land on me
>   again, Lord.
So goodbye, good boy.

THE MARCH OF COXEY'S ARMY

Massillon, Ohio, to Washington
—March 24 to May 1, 1894

They started on Easter Sunday like resurrected nobodies.
It was snowing into the chuck wagons, into the split drum
        and the tubas.
Before they blew out of town, someone counted a hundred noses.
    The taverns were shut as tight as a Presbyterian,
        And respectable doors were latched and keyholes corked all
            over Massillon
        Which on Sunday wouldn't even spell sarsaparilla in front of
            a deacon.
They came from all over the dusty map, gimp-legged and
        tatterdemalion,
Out of work, out at heels, out of boxcars, weak from eating
        slumgullion,
Ready to walk from Hell to breakfast and from breakfast to
        Washington.
        Two million men that winter were standing in bread-lines
        While gentlemen sucked their teeth and twiddled their gold
            watch-chains,
        Havanas between muttonchops, vests covered with dollar
            signs.
General Jacob Coxey from his carriage saw a country managed by
        halfwits,
By boodlers and credit-jugglers and quick-silver plutocrats,
Coupon-clippers and shufflers of imaginary banknotes.
        He saw the banks were scratching out confidence money
        Which stood for dollars whenever they didn't have any
        Or which stood for nothing whenever the banks felt slippery.
His daughter Mamie was bawling in the attic because she had to
        stay home.
Jesse, his son, was galloping around in an old Civil War uniform.
His grim wife rode in a carriage, rocking the baby Legal Tender
        in one arm.
        The buglers and astrologers, Chicago cowboys and Toledo
            Indians started off
        Behind Greasy Browne (his sombrero, his beard, and his
            manifesto the color of snuff)

102

With "The Dog Who Never Deserts the Flag" chained to the
    flagstaff.
From first to last, each footstep, each turn of a wagonwheel
Was a lurch from brick to rock, from rut to mudhole.
The road went east, and the wind came west to freeze its whistle.
    At first the band played "After the Ball Is Over" smack on
        the beat,
    But you can't march to a waltz unless you've got three feet,
    So they boomed and blared "Where Is My Wand'ring Boy
        Tonight?"
They had no bombs, but most had beards and nearly a dozen had
    overcoats,
And they all had lank faces and underfed gullets.
The general said, "Congress tears up pieces of paper, not Petitions
    in Boots!"
    The first mile, the first noon, the first night, men sat down to
        mull it over
    And didn't catch up. But others came, and like a sluggish
        river
    The march went on, though it was always different water.
The snow got tired and quit. And evening after evening
Sheriffs and paunchy deputies came out to keep them going
Sore foot after foot to the nearest county line.
    They looked at the freezing farms and the melting houses,
    They looked at people by the road, and people looked back
        with uncertain faces.
    At night they looked for stars, but saw the ends of their noses.
And they were surprised each morning under the baggy tents
To find each other there, eating hardtack, hitching up their pants,
And suddenly they had no room for lap-dogs, taffy-pullers, and
        house-plants.
    The wealthy General wore his homburg, foulard tie, and
        morning trousers
    And didn't try rednecking his way around the workers.
    And he slept in hotels on the march and not on cinders.
But he had them chanting, "Work for the Unemployed and Food
        for the Indigent!"
And "If Banks Let Us Down, We're Up to the Government!"
And "We're Sunk If We Keep Inflating and Money Doesn't!"
    And "The Unemployed Can Make Gardens Out of
        Battlegrounds!"
    And "The Unemployed Can Build Highways If Nobody Ties
        Their Hands!"

And "He Rose On Easter, But Death To Interest On Bonds!"
Were they out of their minds? They were out of the State of Ohio,
       heading down
Where smoke was exploding like shellfire on the horizon,
To a blistered valley where the air stood thick as policemen.
       Men burnt the color of pig-iron came out of the half-shut
          mills to wave.
       They stood in somebody else's Homestead, keeping a few
          jobs, staying alive.
       And the companies minded everyone's manners with the
          business-end of a sheriff.
The marchers kept their heads for miles between silent rows
Of loaded militia who were aching to keep the peace,
While newspapers shouted, A PLAGUE OF LOCUSTS and
       A MARCH OF DISEASE!
       And somehow they didn't catch typhus on the banks of the
          Ohio.
       Sometimes the river would back up, sometimes it would flow.
       It was close enough to smell, but too thick to jump into.
And Greasy Browne shouted, "A thousand bums going in one
       direction instead of nowhere!
A thousand bums with their stomachs growling for supper!
If we had a thousand bums, we'd raise a stink like a pillar of fire!"
       And "If every gun in the country backfired, you wouldn't
          scratch a bum."
       And "Give every bum a bath and a haircut, and kill your
          society column."
       And "The General's the Cerebrum of Christ and I'm the
          Cerebellum!"
He could give an evangelical chalk-talk that doubled up reporters.
He painted the haloed head of Christ on one of his posters
And gave it calculating, squinty eyes and his own whiskers.
       But the General said, "When your belly's empty, you can't
          stand belly-laughs.
       Laughs won't pull Congressmen's pig-knuckles out of their
          troughs.
       And you can't blow down their marble pig-pens with huffs
          and puffs."
In photographs, they slump in their bowlers and striped shirts,
Shaving each other or strewn under canvas like a wrecked circus.
But as the weeks crawled by, they crawled slowly southeast.
       There lay the Allegheny Mountains crumpled like soggy
          cardboard.

Men came and men quit, but there were two hundred
    Scraping themselves uphill, even when the wind turned solid.
They felt forgotten, but got over it and into Maryland
Through snowdrifts and insurrections, leaving behind
Reporters, unbroken windows, live chickens, old clothes, and
        friends.
    They lived off the uneasy land, breaking some laws
    Like trespassing, parading without permits, and thinking on
        Sundays.
    When they came to the last river, they were headline news.
They spent two days and two nights in barges on the Potomac
Till their faces looked greener than Martha Washington's on a
        greenback.
Each could have thrown a silver dollar across, if he'd had it in his
        stomach.
    But they grew fresher and brighter, tramping toward
        Washington.
    When they camped on the last of April, five hundred strong,
    They dusted their hair, stiffened their backs, and cranked up
        the dawn.
The ranks were loaded with Secret Servicemen,
Spies, and pipe-sucking Pinkerton agents, according to Greasy
        Browne.
The General said, "They've come to school, they'll stay for
        graduation."
    President Grover Cleveland stood up and started smoking.
    Senator William Jennings Bryan sat down and stopped
        talking.
    But Brigadier General Ordway ordered everyone to start
        countermarching.
"No parades and no banners," said the D. of C. Chief of Police,
But here came runaway Mamie Coxey dressed as the Goddess of
        Peace
With 30,000 people cheering and her hair tickling her knees.
    She was shocking her mother at the bottom of her bent,
    And the band was booming "Marching Through Georgia"
        with an Ohio accent,
    Yet the marchers were as good as gold when they passed the
        Mint.
They wanted to go to the Capitol steps and hear the General
        speak,
But suddenly there was a straight wall of policemen on horseback,
One for each marcher and some left over, each twirling a
        nightstick.

Adjusting his pince-nez and saying, "Excuse me, please,"
The General cut to his left and, zigzagging like Congress,
Crossed to the Capitol steps on a carpet of grass.
His speech was still in his hand when he was arrested.
"Here's where Kings and Princes have wiped their feet," it said.
"Here's where the fat-necked lobbyists have been red-carpeted."
And hundreds of billyclubs went up and came down
On scalps and derbies, on temples and collarbones.
When the dust blew off, "The Dog Who Never Deserts the
Flag" had broken its chain.
And the march was going in all directions, into poolrooms and
hospitals,
Into taverns and city parks, into boxcars and jails,
Into the air, into the backs of minds. It was scattered like
handbills.
People strolled home or went groggy to dinner.
Some looked at the blood. Some looked at themselves. Some
looked at 1894.
The General got twenty days for walking on the grass, and
the show was over.

SEARCHING IN THE BRITANNIA TAVERN

to Earl Lund, Clallam Tribe, Washington

To get to the land of the dead, you must go through
The place where everything is flying, past falling water
To the curb, across the sidewalk, stumbling, to the hunting
    ground;
Sleeping by day and moving only by night, you will come
To the place where you must sink, then rise, then enter
The abrupt silence where they have hidden your soul.

Having no one to be, the dead steal souls. They lie
In wait in the middle of the floor, or spraddle for balance,
Their eyes burnt out. Those climbing toward the door
Have never entered. Those descending never arrive. They stand
Facing in different directions, blinking at walls, remembering
Nothing about your life. Remember, you told me,

Only your spirit can grapple with the dead.
It must be danced or it never appears. You must watch for it
At night, or walk all day in your sleep, or stay under water
To make it come to you. When it enters, nothing stands still.
The wall is the floor, the floor and ceiling are walls,
Its voice is breaking in your ears, its broken speech

Is saying what you must know, the dead are falling
Against each other, rattling their helpless fingers, remember,
The First People changed into bears, into rocks and fish,
Into trees, beavers, and birds, when they learned that men
    were coming,
And there, stalking toward you, the dark one is
    Tah-mah-no-us,
One Who Has Never Changed, his terrible mouth is smiling,
    he bears
Your soul slowly toward you in cupped hands.

GETTING OUT OF JAIL ON MONDAY

I'm going into the building, he's coming out.
It's City Property where official cement
Pours sideways, up, and down out of the windows.
I'm paying fines for driving and walking crooked
And he's getting out of jail on a fine morning,
Singing and waving, just walking away.

As if he'd sung my name, I turn and follow
This husky, bowlegged, upright, sockless Indian
Who's singing, going downhill as straight as an arrow.
He's chanting deep in his throat, his mouth hangs open
Like that tavern doorway. Stomping, he sings against it
As harsh and sharp as the wind through underbrush.

The sun is sunnyside up, swatches of sky
Are glancing down from the windows around us,
The gutter's a foot away, the secretaries
Are sharpening the corners of their eyes,
The boards are busy upstairs, good signatures
Are flourishing at the business-ends of letters,

And the Indian goes inside like a parade.
Me too. I buy him a beer. He sings around it,
Staring at me with flat obsidian eyes,
Then drinks it aloud. The sun is over easy.
I buy another, we down it against the clock
Which is prying the hour apart with its bare hands.

All over town the time-vaults are yawning open.
They disengage their polished, case-hardened teeth
From the dark strikes that bolted them all home.
The money is rolling out into the morning
After a breathless weekend in the tank.
The jukebox crackles and burns in the corner.

I give him my necktie. He threads it like a belt
And hikes his pants, cinching himself tight.
We try to imagine not being arrested
Till the end of the week. I tell him about work,
And we drink to cinches tighter than our luck.
Outside, the sun is a raw egg in a beer,

108

And the cars and cabs are jerking around noon.
From this enormous distance, you have to shout
To make yourself heard. You have to pay a fine
For singing or shouting crooked at a machine.
With five days off and two in a safe place,
We're like an investment. The Indian backs me up.

He backs me up against the front of the tavern
And does a dance with his hair in his face. I explain
To people scuttling around him what he means.
He means he's working at dancing through the week
And staring at the burnt insides of eyelids
With a stomach full of the City and no socks.

Machines are cranking mimeographed Tuesdays,
Tuesdays are sticking to Wednesdays, they're running
        off Thursdays
In case of increased demand, but Fridays go blank,
And trying to see Friday west of Monday
Takes an Indian's eyes. It's over the brow of the hill
Like the U.S. Cavalry with its spit and tarnish,

And suddenly dancing, I'm Big Medicine.
I prophesy: Nothing is going to work
Till it sings for itself. Hundreds of want-ads
Are flying from Pioneer Square to Puget Sound
Like seagulls. The beak of Thunderbird is breaking
On Killer Whale, we all light up in the rain,

And it puts us out. The sun is scrambling off.
The Indian rattles away through a strange language.
Slowly my arches sink back to the pavement.
My hair sits down, my chin warps shut like a drawer.
I put the touch on myself and start uphill,
A solid citizen, going to pay on time.

THE BURGLAR

Being a burglar, you slip out of doors in the morning
And look at the street by looking at the sky,
Not being taken in by anything blue.
You must look to the left or right to see across.
If nothing strikes your eye, if no one comes running,
You've stolen another day.

You must spend it on your toes
At the edges of buildings, doorways, and windows
Wherever no one is watching close enough.
Keep your fingers light as smoke.
You may have permission to kiss with one eye open.
Try every door while leaning away from it.

But sundown is serious; it's time to go home
To the house that will draw you under its empty wing.
Climbing like ivy up the drains, go through
The furthest window into a dark room.
Wait there to hear how everything has gone.
Then, masking every motion,

Glide to the stairwell.
They will be eating dinner: the man and the woman
At opposite ends of a white and silver table;
Between them, food and candles and children.
Their knives and forks go in and out of their mouths;
Whatever they do will aim them toward each other.

Now, follow your fingerprints around all corners
From nightlatch to velvet lid, from hasp to stone.
Everything locked, of course, has been locked for you:
You must break in softly, take whatever you find
Whether you understand what it is or not.
Breathe in, reach out,

Stealing one thing at a time.
If you grow hungry, thinking of their desserts,
It's time to vanish over the windowsill.
You must go without their dinner into the night,
Not saying goodbye, not waiting to scrawl a note
To say you're running away, but running away.

THE SHOPLIFTER

She stands alone in the aisle, head tilted
As if listening to women, the women
Glittering or moping past her
Among the gloves and purses, glancing like light
On necklaces, half clear, half dreaming.

Everyone is here; no one is watching—
Children and loud mothers, the girls in black,
The manager erect among questions.
Languidly her hand moves
Over the counter. Now it is touching

Something, lifting it, taking, and hiding.
Wherever it goes now, she darkens it.
She walks along the rows to the blurred
Revolving door, turning herself out.
The sun is melting like wax over the sidewalk.

Now a man stops her, holds her tightly.
A flush comes up across her face like a veil.
He brings her back alive; his hand
Is firm on her elbow, leading her up the aisle.
No one is here, but everyone is watching.

She is floating sideways, being drawn
Into the ceremonious distance, away from us.
Rising along the stairway, looking back,
She smiles serenely against the light.
The shop is lifting, lifting itself with her.

THE HOLD-UP

First comes a fence, then the mouth of an alley,
Then a shadow on the other side of shadows
Becomes a pole, a doorway, a garbage can
Becoming a bush with a voice becoming an arm
Holding a gun at my back. This is a hold-up.
We wait a moment. We listen
For whatever it might be I'm going to say.
The wind crawls out from under the parked cars.

My arms go up in the air. My hands turn white.
Apparently I won't be saying anything.
He empties the deep pocket over my heart,
Then pats my hips as if guessing my weight.
Half-turning, I see the stocking down his face
Erasing lips and eyes, smoothing his nose.
We pass the time of night together.
He does the breathing for both of us.

The muzzle touches my back
Gently, like the muzzle of a dog. What's holding me up?
Take off your shoes. I stand in stocking feet
On the cinders. He begins to fade.
I had been walking from streetlight to streetlight,
My shadow straight as a footbridge under me,
Forgetting the mouths of alleys by moonlight.
My shoes and my money are running away in the dark.

THE VISITING HOUR

Strip off your clothes and give them to a man
In a uniform, hurry to take a shower,
Put on a starchy, stark-white coverall
That can stand up by itself, then keeping in line,
March to the visitor's room.

It has lamps, rugs, curtains, movable furniture,
And a woman among some women, looking at you
And wearing a dress and holding out her arms
 (Which may be entered against her)
And shutting and opening her mouth for an hour.

Standing behind his bullet-proof glass, the guard
Has been instructed to stare, but stares at the wall,
The ceiling, or between your bodies
As if recalling games on television.
What you can do is act like him for her:

Your eyes must look at something common between you—
A crack, a flower on a cushion.
Your hands may touch each other item by item
In order, checking down the list of reminders.
You may reach for almost anything but conclusions.

When a bell rings, there is nothing left to answer,
No one is calling or waiting, nothing is ready—
The time has simply gone, and the time has come
To say goodbye like scouts of opposing factions
From opposite closing doors.

From the corridor, you'll enter an empty room
To be stripped and searched for imaginary objects:
Stooping, squatting, and squinting, the guards go through
Your closets and blind alleys
To catch you keeping what you can never get.

The long way back will take you past a gate
Where you can see a man outside in a tower.
His searchlight, his eyes, his rifle

All turn toward you if you stop to wave.
He must know you to let you out. He doesn't know you.

And in Cell Block D, nobody wants to shoot you.
Those tiers with railings
Rise forty feet like the face of a motel
With ice on every floor. Like venetian blinds,
The catwalks show you mounting, kneeling, or lying.

The guards in the gallery simply look and listen
Over their sights if you thumb your nose or scream
Or try to throw something far enough to reach them.
They'll put your name on a list; then visitors
Will have to imagine you for years and years.

THE ESCAPE ARTIST

for Will Desmond

In the middle of the crowd, they're strapping him into it,
Straining and buckling as if over a madman.
Through the tapering, cuffless sleeves of the strait-jacket
He hugs himself to keep his body waiting.
The crane hums loudly between buildings. It hoists
The heavy hook between the straps at his ankles.
He smiles Goodbye, Goodbye, going upside down,
Red in the face, his hair standing on end.
The crowd below makes room for a mistake.

Hooked in the clear sky, he dangles
Like something restless dreaming about flying.
Inside the canvas, suddenly his forearms
Wrestling his sidling shoulders, his raw neck heaving
And doubling, everything writhing—his head comes
        breaching out
From the crooks of his elbows,
The buckles parting; his chest and arms break free
And he hangs flapping, a wet, half-folded moth.

From the street, nervous advice. Someone baits him.
Flashguns. Mouths gape as if being fed.
He peels himself, dropping the empty jacket.
The sweat rolls up his face and into his eyes
Like tears coming backward; his smile is wrong side up.
Slowly the cable lowers him on the hook,
Putting him back where he was, among us.

TUMBLEWEED

Here comes another, bumping over the sage
Among the greasewood, wobbling diagonally
Downhill, then skimming a moment on edge,
Tilting lopsided, bouncing end over end
And springing from the puffs of its own dust
To catch at the barbed wire
And hang there, shaking, like a riddled prisoner.

Half the sharp seeds have fallen from this tumbler,
Knocked out for good by head-stands and pratfalls
Between here and wherever it grew up.
I carry it in the wind across the road
To the other fence. It jerks in my hands,
Butts backward, corkscrews, lunges and swivels,
Then yaws away as soon as it's let go,
Hopping the scrub uphill like a kicked maverick.
The air goes hard and straight through the wires and
    weeds.
Here comes another, flopping among the sage.

THE SOLES

The soles are lying in shallows off Dungeness Spit.
They rest on vacant sides and stare at the sun.
Their skin like sand is glowing against the sand.

The tide has come and gone. It comes again.
The soles are lying still as their own breath.
The ocean passes through the straits of their gills.

One eye has moved an inch in a million years
To join the other on the burning side,
Drawn up like a moon from underlying night.

They dart and bury themselves as we drift over.
They cloud the sand across their speckled halves.
Their fixed, their wandering eyes stare up again.

RECOLLECTION

Dear, I have been days
Drudging at words. They lie
Wherever I put them down
As separate as stones.
There on the page, they are
Exactly what they are.

Only an hour ago
I was driving from nowhere
To nowhere in my car
When I remembered you—
As simply, as obviously
As men remember food
And turn from breaking stones
On stones, to break their bread.

This is the whole truth.
I stopped, and I sat down
On cinders, held my head
Together, took a drink
Of the unmanageable air
Where we first caught our breath,
And made this out of love.

FIRE BY THE RIVER

We gather wood, the bleached, clay-covered branches
As heavy as fossils, drag them to the shore,
    And cross them, touching a match
To a nest of twigs. And the fire begins between us
Under this evening kindled by our breath.

It gathers dusk in tight against our backs,
Lighting us half by half. The river roars
    Like a fire drawn through a valley.
The smoke pours down to the water's edge like a creek
And empties into the broad, downstreaming night.

The first chill draws our arms around each other.
Like firelight under eyelids, the stars spread out.
    We lie down with ourselves.
The lighted halves of our bodies sink together.
The moon leans inward, banking on darkness.

Set free by our sleep and coming down to the water,
The bears, the deer, the martens dark as their fur,
    As soundless as night herons,
All drink and turn away, making no light.
The tail of the wind is stirring the soft ashes,

And nothing of ours will be left in the morning
Though we guard it now through dewfall and ground
       mist.
    But here at the heart of night
A salmon leaps: the smack of his wild body
Breaks through the valley, splashing our sleep with fire.

NINE CHARMS AGAINST THE HUNTER

In the last bar on the way to your wild game,
May the last beer tilt you over among friends
And keep you there till sundown—failing that,
A breakdown on the road, ditching you gently
Where you may hunt for lights and a telephone.
Or may your smell go everywhere through the brush,
Upwind or crosswind. May your feet come down
Invariably crunching loudly on dry sticks.
Or may whatever crosses your hairlines—
The flank of elk or moose, the scut of a deer,
The blurring haunch of a bear, or another hunter
Gaping along his sights at the likes of you—
May they catch you napping or freeze you with buck fever.
Or if you fire, may the stock butting your shoulder
Knock you awake around your bones as you miss,
Or then and there, may the noise pour through your mind
Imaginary deaths to redden your daydreams:
Dazed animals sprawling forward on dead leaves,
Thrashing and kicking, spilling themselves as long
As you could wish, as hard, as game,
And then, if you need it, imaginary skinning,
Plucking of liver and lights, unraveling guts,
Beheading trophies to your heart's content.
Or if these charms have failed and the death is real,
May it fatten you, hour by hour, for the trapped hunter
Whose dull knife beats the inside of your chest.

IN THE OPEN SEASON

By what stretch of the mind had we come there, lurching
    and crackling
Mile after mile uphill through the ruts and ice-lidded
    chuckholes
On the logging road, the pine boughs switching across our
    windows?
It was the middle of gray-green daylight when we stalled,
    then climbed
On foot into scraggy clearings, while blue and ruffed
    grouse
Went booming and rocketing slapdash deep under the
    branches
Beside us, beating our hearts, and the guns began slamming
Their blunt, uninterrupted echoes from valley to valley.
We zigzagged up through the stunted hemlocks, over
    stumps and snow
Into shale, into light, to a ridgecrest frozen hard as a
    backbone
And, lying down as if breathing our last, caught the air
One burst at a time. When the world came back, we looked
At dozens of miles of it crumbling away from us
Where bears and deer were spilling out of hiding.
The overlapping thumps of shotgun and rifle
Froze us around each other out of the wind
Where frost had grown on itself, thicker than moss,
In spires and spikelets like a bed of nails
Under our backs by turns. And the light broke out
Of everything we touched in bristling spectrums,
And we felt the day break over again
And again, snow blowing across the sun
To dazzle our half-closed eyes.
But the earth shivered with guns
Below us—the birds, the bears,
And the deer bleeding toward sundown.
We touched each other's wounds
Like star-crossed, stir-crazed lovers
Dying again and again.

ARCHEOLOGICAL NOTES

Wherever they put their feet, the herdsmen beyond bleak
    Astrakhan
Scuffle in flint chips older than all arrows.
Past the concrete end of a runway in Seattle, bulldozers
    found
The sprawled, imponderable bones of a giant sloth.
Men stamping their feet for their lives in Rome have fallen
Down through the hollow streets to catacombs.
Under the flights of rain, clay dogs, clay men come
    tumbling
Into Oaxaca valleys like messages.
Digging for worms in Saratoga Springs, boys unearth
    muskets
And buckles, the green brass of revolutions.
In cities like kitchen middens, men crack the halves of
    themselves
And then go rich in a heap to be lived on.
Where I grew up—in a swamp east of Chicago—if you stamp
    your foot,
You stay right where you are and what you are:
Ditch-diggers in bogs and slag find nothing but Prohibition
    Man—
Thick skulls, gold teeth, and pointed preserved shoes.

THE WARBLER

My neighbor shut off his engine at the curb,
But as we talked, it started chirping and squeaking
Like a rusty ghost. We raised the hood and looked:
A half-grown warbler clung to a hood-brace,
Its beak still broad and yellow for feeding,
Gray-yellow powdered under its blunt wings.
It shifted tight to my finger, ruffled its down,
Then hunched and flew without a trace of a tail
All the way over the street, flew straight and hard
But downward, flopping and rolling
Finally among the roots of an elm.
I picked it up. It looked as good as new.

To make a story short, it died in the morning,
Having eaten nothing, having turned away
From eyedroppers and bugs on the ends of toothpicks,
Still chirping for something else we couldn't find
Like the nest it fell out of. My neighbor had driven
All over town that morning, noticing nothing.

I want to remember what we didn't see:
The warbler falling, for some damned reason or other,
And being fed or not being fed in the gutter
With a car stretched over it like a stormy arbor,
Then hopping from street to kingpin to shock-absorber
Over the fuel pump to a snarl of wires
To a slit of light where the hood and fender flange,
Jounced up and down, being waggled in a nest
Of pistons pecking their exploding chambers,
The horns in its ears like apocalyptic geese,
The engine roaring like a pterodactyl,
The endlessly belted fan whirling its wings
In the darkness. When those died down at our house,
It went on chirping its single demanding note.

FROM HELL TO BREAKFAST

Leaving the night upstairs
And minding their manners,
They sit down at the table.
For what they are about
To receive, God, make them grateful
And good enough to eat.
What made these appetites?—
Tomato juice for vampires,
Heaps of scrambled eggs
While the rooster is still crowing.
And what's the use of letting
The night into the morning?
Stir sugar and cream in it.

Their eyes are the right colors
Except at the corners, their clothes
Are as cool as the season,
She put her face on straight,
He had a close shave, but they seem
To remember someone screaming.
Was it next door? In the street?
She dreamed something was burning
In the oven, a midnight snack
No one would dare to eat.
On stumps like a veteran,
Something walked in his sleep
Like himself cut down to size.

Give them their daily bread
And the daily paper. Hundreds
Were screaming if they had time:
Some fell or were pushed, and some
Ran smack into it
Or woke up behind bars.
Thousands coughed up their souls
In the night, and two got in
On the wrong side of bed
And cured their love like meat.

They both may be excused
If they wipe their mouths. Look,

No hands across the table, no
Holes in the walls, no windows
Scattered across the floor.
It could have been worse, and they
Could have been worse than it.
They have each other's names
On their shopping lists. In the doorway,
A brief passage of arms,
And they're off, they're off and running.

CROSSING HALF A RIVER

Stretching and heaving behind me, the snarled wilderness
Of crags as high as buildings, hanging valleys,
Paths cut by deadfalls,
And cracks where cedars cling for their lives, hogbacks and
    spurs
Where no one comes or goes by his own choice—
But here, an island in a river.
The shore, broadened by summer, shelves down to the
    quick water.
Hobbling, I come to the edge. A foot away
The fingerling salmon dart,
Then hover. In the riverbed the stones turn bright as birds,
Splashed, speckled like eggs or the breasts of fledglings.
Being shaken in my boots,
I start across as deep as my knees—hearing the rush
Of the milk-blue water coming down from snow—
As deep as my leaning thighs;
And the downstream leg must lead the way, groping and
    yawing
As it reaches ahead, the upstream leg coming level
In line with the current
For shelter. In the deep channel, this body—tilted,
    half-buoyant,
Unsure of itself, its feet at cross purposes—
Gives up its footholds lightly,
Halved by a horizontal storm and a vertical sun,
Head swimming with light and arms like stubs of fins
Fishing for balance.
Then slowly it finds itself: more surely the feet step down
On time pulled tight below them, not coming sideways;
They wallow ashore
On the downstream spit like castaways. The dividing river
Curves down its forks, riffling and whitening
Or smoothing deep in pools.
Far off, the upstream point is a jumble of head-sized stones,
But halfway here, on the spine of the bare island,
Gnarled by flooding winters,
Heaped with its own leaves, with the drifted rubble of
    seasons,
A clutch of willows like a broken garden

Begins living and dying,
Still separate, but slowly bringing a world together
With what can still be counted on my fingers,
With white-crowned sparrows
And mourning doves, with pipers and killdeer, with
    whatever
Comes to be caught at flood stage in the rains
When only the bent willows
Will keep their place above the crest of the river,
    beginning—
Like all I wanted to say—with sticks and stones
When thought first stuttered
Against the current. I recognize myself by the water,
Now going into the water toward the shore,
Now dreaming myself across.

STRETCHING

Leaving the road and crossing the hard shoulder
And walking on washed-out clay, having to zigzag
From sage to bunch grass to prickly pear to bones
A half-mile over the prairie to a butte
The size of a ruin— (the sun is crackling sideways
As straight, as dry, as thick as the wind
That's fallen flat on the ground this evening) —

In the wrong clothes, at the wrong time of day,
I come to the crumbling limestone foot:
There's no way up but up the pitching chimneys
Thirty rough feet to the crest. I climb them, passing
A disembodied rattle between rocks
Which means keep going or don't keep going,

And then I'm standing somewhere in Montana
South of Lame Deer, raw kneed, raw handed,
In a place I couldn't invent, in an old place,
On the sparse grass untouched by buffalo,
On table-rock half eaten by weather, the black-

And-white lark buntings skimming past stones
Heaped in a head-high cairn in the middle of nowhere,
Where someone came and waited once, then changed
Into wind and rain, into grass, sunlight, and dirt,

Which come and go, crossing each other out
In a heap as permanent as a landscape,
A place to be promised something bleak as years,

Where my hands and knees feel ready for a change,
Where giving up is perfectly natural,

Where giving back goes far as the eye can stretch.

LAST LOOK

for Vernon Watkins—d. Seattle,
Oct. 1967

He was crossing a bridge when I saw him last,
A pack on his back, his gray hair glistening
In the rain. He was looking toward the mountains
Where the salmon in the channel under his feet
Were going that gray October.
His pack was full of books; he was starting home,
Eyes turning against the current toward high snow
As clearly, as naturally
As the eyes of the homing salmon under him.

NOTE FROM BODY TO SOUL

Each word a rock
The size of a fist—
I throw them one by one
At the dark window.

PLAINSONG FOR EVERYONE WHO
WAS KILLED YESTERDAY

You haven't missed anything yet:
One dawn, one breakfast, and a little weather,
The clamor of birds whose names
You didn't know, perhaps some housework,
Homework, or a quick sale.
The trees are still the same color,
And the Mayor is still the mayor, and we're not
Having anything unusual for lunch.
No one has kissed her yet
Or slept with him. Our humdrum lives
Have gone on humming and drumming
Through one more morning.

But for a while, we must consider
What you might have wished
To do or look like. So far,
Thinking of you, no one has forgotten
Anything he wanted to remember.
Your death is fresh as a prize
Vegetable—familiar but amazing,
Admirable but not yet useful—
And you're in a class
By yourself. We don't know
Quite what to make of you.

You've noticed you don't die
All at once. Some people like me
Still offer you our songs
Because we don't know any better
And because you might believe
At last whatever we sing
About you, since no one else is dreaming
Of singing: *Remember that time
When you were wrong? Well, you were right.
And here's more comfort: all fires burn out
As quickly as they burn. They're over
Before we know it, like accidents.*

You may feel you were interrupted
Rudely, cut off in the middle

Of something crucial,
And you may even be right
Today, but tomorrow
No one will think so.
Today consists of millions
Of newsless current events
Like the millions of sticks and stones
From here to the horizon. What are you
Going to miss? The calendar
Is our only program.

Next week or next year
Is soon enough to consider
Those brief occasions you might rather
Not have lost: the strange ones
You might go so far
As to say you could have died for:
Love, for example, or all
The other inflammations of the cerebral
Cortex, the astounding, irreversible
Moments you kept promising yourself
To honor, which are as far away
Now as they always were.

THE APOTHEOSIS OF THE GARBAGEMEN

And they come back in the night through alleys to find us
By the clashing of raised lids,
By garage doors' lifted heads, the swung gates, the bottomless
Galvanized cans on their shoulders,
In luminous coveralls
They follow the easy directions on boxes, scattering
Bushels of brown grass and apple cores,
Old candy wrappers folded around sweet nothings,
And sacks with their stains on fire,
They are coming through hedges, dragging geometry
In a dark clutch of rainbows,
See, the smashed jars
Prinked out with light, and the vacuum bags
Bursting their dust in the night like the phantasms of horseflies,
Through the burning bacon fat
Their baseball caps go flying, their feet
As solid as six-packs on the lawn, the slam-bang of their coming
Sending the lettuce leaves against our windows
Like luna moths, the marrow whistling
Out of the wishbones of turkeys, the husks and rinds,
The lost-wax castings of corncobs and teabags,
The burnt-out lightbulbs pulsing in midair,
The coupons filled out
With our last names for all the startling offers,
Oh see, their hands are lifted by the gloves
Untying the knots in plastic bags, to catch
The half-burnt ashes raining around their heads,
The crusts and empties.
As the skeletons of lampshades catch at the first light,
They are going back in their empty trucks and singing
To the dump, to the steaming rust
In the rolling, hunch-backed, beckoning earth,
The sea of decay where our foundering fathers
Rubbled their lives,
They have found the way
Back to God's plenty, to rags and riches,
But will come back to us with all we could wish for
In the darkness, singing love and wild appetite,
The good rats and roaches,
The beautiful hogs and billygoats dancing around them.

133

from
RIVERBED
(1972)

RIVERBED

1

Through the salt mouth of the river
They come past the dangling mesh of gillnets
And the purse-mouthed seines, past the fishermen's last strands
By quarter-light where the beheaded herring
Spiral against the tide, seeing the shadowy others
Hold still, then slash, then rise to the surface, racked
And disappearing—now deepening slowly
In the flat mercurial calm of the pulp mills, groping
Half clear at last and rising like the stones below them
Through swifter and swifter water, the salmon returning
By night or morning in the white rush from the mountains,
Hunting, in the thresh and welter of creek mouths
And shifting channels, the one true holding place.

Out of our smoke and clangor, these miles uphill,
We come back to find them, to wait at their nesting hollows
With the same unreasoning hope.

2

We walk on round stones, all flawlessly bedded,
Where water drags the cracked dome of the sky
Downstream a foot at a glance, to falter there
Like caught leaves, quivering over the sprint
Of the current, the dashing of surfaces.

In a month of rain, the water will rise above
Where we stand on a curving shelf below an island—
The blue daylight scattered and the leaves
All castaways like us for a season.
The river turns its stones like a nesting bird
From hollow to hollow. Now gulls and ravens
Turn to the salmon stranded among branches.

They lie in the clear shallows, the barely dead,
While some still beat their flanks white for the spawning,
And we lie down all day beside them.

THE FISHERMAN'S WIFE

When she said, "No,"
I freed the hook, holding the two-foot rainbow
With both hands over the dock-side in the water.
Its mouth would scarcely move
Though I scooped it, belly down, below the surface
Again and again to rouse it.
Hoping too soon, I let it go. It tilted,
Beginning to slide out of sight, its tailfin stiff.

Again, she said, "No." Before I could take her place,
She had stepped casually in her summer dress
Into the lake and under, catching the trout
And coming upward, cradling it in her arms.
Then breathing less than it, not shutting her eyes,
She settled slowly under water, her face
As calm as that water deep below the cedars.

I caught her by the hair, bringing her back
Alive. The trout slid loose, its red-and-silver side
Flashing beyond her, down into the dark.
I saw the tail flick once before it faded.

I helped her up. She stared at me, then the water.
We sat on edge till the moon came out, but nothing
Rose, belly up, to mock it at our feet.

THE KEEPERS

The drizzle and wind had driven the keepers
Indoors at the marine aquarium.
We stood between the seals and the whale tank,
Our games rained out like theirs.

But she climbed to the round catwalk
Ahead of me, and there was the sleek half-grown
Black-and-white killer whale, being heaved
And lapped by its own backwash.

I couldn't have closed my arms
Around its head, and wouldn't have dreamed
Of trying. It swam in a flat circle,
Surging, as though pacing a cage.

At the opposite side she knelt, held out her hand
Over the gray water, and called
Something I couldn't hear in the wind.
The whale went there and lifted its dark head

And opened its mouth a foot below
As wide as a window. From among the glistening
Perfectly pointed teeth there came
A thick blunt tongue as pink as a mollusc's foot.

She kissed it, as God is my witness. The whale
Sank back and swam as it had before.
She came toward me at the top of the stair,
As I braced against the wind blowing between us,

And offered me those same lips to be kissed.
And something I hadn't dared
Believe in, something deep as my salt
Rose to the surface of my mouth to touch them.

139

IN THE BADLANDS

When we fell apart in the Badlands and lay still
As naked as sunlight
On the level claybed among the broken buttes,
We were ready for nothing—
The end of the day or the end of our quick breathing,
The abolishment of hearts—
And saw in the sky a dozen vultures sailing
With our love as the pivot.
They had come in our honor, invited by what could pass
In their reckoning
For the thresh and crux and sprawled languor of death,
Too much pale skin
In that burning bed where we lay at our own banquet,
Being taken in
As thoroughly as the fossils under us
When they lay down;
And the sea that once was there welled up in our eyes
For the sake of the sun.

TALKING BACK

This green-and-red, yellow-naped Amazon parrot, Pythagoras,
Is the master of our kitchen table. *Every good boy*
Does fine! he shouts, hanging upside down, and *Pieces of eight*
And gold doubloons! in his cage whose latches he picked with ease
Till we bought a padlock, *To market, to market, to buy a fat pig!*
Home again, home again, and he rings his brass bell, as militant
As salvation, or knocks his trapeze like a punching bag with his
    beak
Or outfakes and ripostes the treacherous cluster of measuring
    spoons
Which he pretends are out for his blood. How many times
Have I wished him back in his jungle? Instead, he brings it here
Daily with a voice like sawgrass in raucous counterpoint
To after-work traffic, washing machines, or electric razors
As he jangles back at motors in general, *Who knows*
What evil lurks in the hearts of men? but then, inscrutably,
Refusing to laugh like The Shadow. When he walks on the table
In a fantailed pigeon-toed shuffling strut, getting a taste
Of formica with his leathery tongue, he challenges me
Each morning to fight for my wife if I dare to come near her,
Ruffling his neck and hunching, beak open, his amber eyes
Contracting to malevolent points. I taught him everything
He knows, practically, *Fair and foul are near of kin!*
Including how to love her as he croons in her soft voice,
I'm a green bird, and how to test me for the dialectic hell of it,
What then? sang Plato's ghost, *What then?* as if I knew
The answer which Yeats in his finite wisdom forgot to teach me.

THE TRAIL HORSE

"If I could get Yeats on a horse, I'd put a new rhythm
into English poetry."

—Ezra Pound

Get on, expecting the worst—a mount like a statue
Or a bucking runaway.
If neither happens, if this bay mare holds still,
Then you're off
The ground, not touching the ground except through her
Four stilted corners
Which now plop up and down as carefully
In the mud by the road
As if those hoofprints behind her were permanent.
You're in the saddle
As she clip-clops up the path on a slack rein,
Her nose leading the way
Under the pine boughs switching like her tail.
Give in. Sit still.
It won't be hard to let her have her head:
It's hers by a neck;
She'll keep it against your geeing, hawing, or whoaing.
This one's been bred
To walk from daybreak to darkness in the mountains
Up trail or down
And will do it without you tomorrow. The apparatus
Cinching and bridling her,
The leather and metal restraints for a prisoner
Who *won't* be convenient,
Who *won't* do what she's told or listen to reason,
Are mostly for show:
For example, take this place you're passing now—
Tall stumps and boulders,
Thirty degrees of slope and a narrow trail—
A time for judgment,
A time for the nice control of cause and effect.
Do you see the flies
Clustered around her eyelids, nipping their salt?
Or the humming wasp
Tossed from her tail to her rump where it sinks in?
Suddenly swivelling
And sliding, jerking tight as a slipknot

And rearing out from under
Arched like a cow and a half humped over the moon,
She leaves you alone,
And you part company on the only terms
Possible: hers being yours—
No straddler of winged horses, no budding centaur,
But a man biting the dust.

THE DEATH AND RESURRECTION
OF THE BIRDS

Falling asleep, the birds are falling
Down through the last light's thatchwork farther than rain,
Their grace notes dwindling
Into that downy pit where the first bird
Waits to become them in the nest of the night.

Silent and featherless,
Now they are one dark bird in darkness.

Beginning again, the birds are breaking
Upward, new-fledged at daybreak, their clapping wingbeats
Striking the sides of the sun, the singing brilliant
Dust spun loose on the wind from the end to the beginning.

DOORS

All over town at the first rattle of night
The doors go shut,
Flat hasp over iron staple, bolt into strike,
Or latch into groove;
And locked and double-locked and burglar-chained,
All of them wait
For the worst, or for morning, steady in their frames:
From hinge to lock stile,
From hard head-casing down to the plinth block,
The doors hang still,
One side for knocking and one for hiding away,
One side for love
And one for crying out loud in the long night
To the pounding heart.

A TOUCH OF THE MOTHER

She stands in the hallway, waiting for a sign
Of breath or smoke, but nothing squeaks the floor
Or whispers at the sink or drifts through transoms.
She has shut the house for the night, but not her eyes:

She threads them up the stairs like the eyes of needles,
Taking a stitch or two, but not in time:
This is the time when all her basting ravels,
When hooks slip out of eyes, and seams come open.

She goes to bed like all good girls and boys
And sisters and husbands by the hands of clocks,
Whether or not those hands will hold her off
Or turn her in or turn her luminous.

Now she must stir her life until it's smooth,
Folding the beaten whiteness through and through
Her mind, like a level cupful taking its place
With all the rich ingredients of the night,

But something chills her. The layers of her dream
Sink in the middle, stiffen, and turn cold:
What is it? Shut the door, the delivery men
Come slouching and lounging into her preserves,

And first you must wash them clean with homemade soap,
Caress them, dry them gently with a towel,
Then soak them for hours in wormwood and witch hazel,
They will fall off and give you no more trouble,

And after turning thick at a rolling boil,
They must form a ball when you drop them in cold water,
Screw the lids hard and store them upside down
In your dark cellar, they will last forever,

And now you know the measure of everything:
Your hand is half as wide as it is long,
Around your wrist is half around your neck,
And twice around your neck is around your waist,

And the cows come back for the leather in your shoes,
The sheep come back for the wool in the tossing blankets,
The geese come back for the feathers in the pillow,
And something blue goes in and out the window.

FOR A MAN WHO DIED IN HIS SLEEP

Once in, he can stay as long as he remembers
To lock the door behind him, being afraid
Of nothing within the ordinary passage
Where he hangs his hat and coat, thinking of bed.

He feels as safe as houses: the predictable ceiling,
The floor at its level best, the walls, the windows
Beyond which the sky, under glass, is slowly streaming
Harmlessly westward with its tricks and shadows,

And going upstairs, he lies down to be soft
In a nest of boxes fitted against the night.
He shuts his lids like theirs and, wrapped like a gift,
Presents himself to sleep, to be opened by daylight.

At first, there is nothing, then something, then everything
Under the doors and over the windowsills
And down the chimney, through the foundation, crawling
From jamb to joist and muttering in the walls,

And he lies tongue-tied under the gaping roof
Through which the weather pours the news of his death:
In sheets and lightning, the broken end of his life
Comes pouring crownfire through the roof of his mouth,

And now he dreams he is dreaming that he knows
His heart's in the right place, safe, beating for good
Against the beams and braces of his house
All the good nights to follow, knocking on wood.

SONG OFFKEY

I needed to make music, but look what's coming:
Something offkey, ungainly, with a rat and a bum in it,
A song like a dish of peaches spilled on the floor
With nothing fitting or touching anything else except by flopping
Slice over juice to meet the linoleum.

Who said there should be a song like a split ragbag?
Nobody needs it—a song with a hole in the middle
Through which some garbled, red-wigged, black-faced gag
Is sticking its head to be conked with baseballs, a song
Like all the wrong weather tangling sunshine and blizzards.

A song should have its tail in its mouth like a hoopsnake,
Or come to a neat point like a stack of belongings,
Or link and labor its opposites in a fixed sword-fight.
Who wants a song like a dump where anything comes or goes?
Here come that rat and that bum for no good reason.

LYING AWAKE IN A BED
ONCE SLEPT IN BY GROVER CLEVELAND

One night, this bed was the Ship of State. It sank
In the middle as deep as its hard slats
Under the burdens of office
Which, pound for pound, were seldom greater,
Sir, than under you. In the midst of panic,
You kept your dignity tight as your fob pocket,
Not throwing your weight around but thinking
Slowly, so slowly they said sometimes
The problems went away while you pondered
Mighty issues, harboring grave doubts.

I picture you that night, on your back
(Giving free sway to your personal corporation)
As if lying in state, with the State
Of New York lying six feet below,
Mulling again the disasters of the body
Politic, making up your mind
After the fact like a teacher grading a newspaper—
Homestead, Haymarket, Pullman, Coxey's Army.

Mr. President, a man like a bed can stand foursquare
For seventy years and have no more
To show for it than a plaque.
Last night, I put myself in your place,
Out flat, my feet jammed at the footboard
Trying to slow things down. Outside,
Beyond a bay window, the same State of New York
(Which had dead bushes and leaves all over it)
Was crawling out from under winter so slowly
I couldn't see it move. Nobody asked me
How to do anything. I wasn't required
To nod or shake. Did the riots happen?
What did I decide? The newspapers haven't come yet,
So I don't know whether we made it through the night.

THE INEXHAUSTIBLE HAT

The incomparable Monsieur Hartz in 1880
Without assistants, with only three small tables
On a well-lit stage produced from a borrowed hat
Seven glass lanterns, each with a lighted candle,
A swaddle of scarves, hundreds of yards of bunting,
A lady's bustle, a stack of empty boxes,
A cage with a lovely, stuffed, half-cocked canary,
A life-size babydoll and dozens of goblets,
A shower of playing cards, a gentleman's wig,
And lastly a grinning skull. Oh Monsieur Hartz,
You were right, you were absolutely right! Encore!

THE EXTRAORDINARY PRODUCTION
OF EGGS FROM THE MOUTH

As he stands alone on stage, the Professor
Shows us he has nothing
Up his sleeve or under his coattails,
Then lowers his brows as seriously as a man
Thinking of being something else, and there,
Would you believe it, from between his lips
The white tip of an egg comes mooning out.

As softly as a hen, he seems to lay it
In his nested fingers. Another. He eggs us on
To laugh and gag for him, to cluck and crow
For the last things we expected or hoped for—
Eggs in both hands, in tophats and fishbowls—
Till he has so many he could quit forever.

But now with a flick of the wrist, seeming to think
Better of his wobbly bonewhite offspring,
He puts one into his mouth, and another,
And each one vanishes back where it came from
Till all his hatchwork has been laid to rest.
He comes to the footlights, gaping for applause,
And except for the pink, withdrawn, quivering tongue,
We see his mouth is absolutely empty.

EPITAPH FOR A LADIES' MAN

His life was dedicated to the proposition.
Girls were his charity, and he gave till it hurt.
Whatever he did to himself was second nature.
First nature now is treating him like dirt.

A VICTORIAN IDYLL

"A gentleman always falls behind his wife in entering the
drawing room. . . . If (the butler) does not know them
by sight, he asks whichever is nearest to him, 'What name,
please?' And whichever one is asked answers, 'Mr. and Mrs.
Lake.' "

—Emily Post, *Etiquette,* p. 350

She came through the room like an answer in long division,
At the top of her form, trailing a dividend.
And when her husband fell down, as he always does,
Flat on his face behind her and met the rug
Like an old friend, we simply sharpened our charcoal.
When the quizzical-looking butler said, "What name, please?"
Someone said wearily, "Mr. and Mrs. Lake."
It's always like this. A few included him
In their sketches as an ambiguous portion
Of the water, but the rest got down to business,
Draping white samite over her rich shoulders
And drawing the sword from their imaginations.

A POLICE MANUAL

"It's not too much of a dull moment, and I'm not in one
place at one time."
                        —Police recruit on NBC News,
                        stating why he liked police work.

As a member of the force, you must consider what force
You will use to defend your streets and citizens
To keep them in working order.
You have your hands, nightstick and whistle, and a gun,
        of course,
But can uphold the law at times by your simple presence,
Implying the power
Structured behind you as solid as penitentiaries
By looking solid and straight and uniform.
You must remember
Complaints are usually the work of the complainers,
And your greatest rewards will come from suspicious persons,
Those who act different,
Who walk too fast or too slow, who avoid your eyes, turn corners
Abruptly and look back, or who ask you silly questions
Over and over
To keep you in one place at a time. You must make them answer
The basic queries of a trade famous for queries—
Who are you? Do you have a license?
Can you walk a straight white line?—But the ambitious
        patrolman prefers
Following in secret. Suppose one climbs a fence,
Crawls into the cellar
Of a deserted factory at midnight and disappears.
Now what do you do? You have suspicions
That law and order
Are being transgressed free of charge. The keeping of the peace
And the protection of property (your luminous guidelines)
Should carry you over
The fence and through the window, regardless of hazards,
After which by following the standard routines
Of search and seizure
You may find him, for instance, boxed in a dark corner,
Looking old and sleepy, proclaiming his innocence.
Officer, officer,
This man begging you of all people to forgive his trespasses

155

Is guilty of breaking and entering for all intents
And purposes, whether
He meant to achieve a felony or not. Your powers
Do not include the granting of privileges
Or exceptions or
The unofficial establishment of sleeping quarters.
The efficient use of a nightstick as an extension
Of your arm and armor
Lies at the heart of patrolling: each human body
Has tender and vulnerable places whose location,
By trial and error,
You may find to your advantage. This man, being down and out,
Is useless except to demonstrate disorder,
So tie up all loose ends.
The mechanics of arrest require a degree of restraint
Which may consist of inflicting deadly wounds
Or touching a sleeve with a finger:
You may take your choice, depending on circumstances.
It's wiser to be the cause of emergencies
Than their prisoner.
No news is good news. The bulk of your daily labors
Will involve the crisp amusements and temptations
That all men long for,
The action, the power, the pursuit of unhappiness.
Fives, tens, and twenties, up to a half a dozen,
Can be folded over
To the size of a matchbook; but the seemingly drab colors
Are instantly recognizable from a distance.
The trouble, therefore,
Is not in finding adequate compensation, but keeping it
From showing too clearly. The rest is in your hands
As a credit to the force.

FORTUNA IMPERATRIX MUNDI

Lady of the turning numbers, our gaudy wheeler, aloft and
        upstage,
   Come down to us now by every ramp and runway
      At our first sign of distress,
Vagina Dentata Immaculata, Matrix of the Plebian Darkness,
    With tassels whirling clockwise and counterclockwise
      From the peaks of your breasts,
Descend and disrobe, lift up our mouths by the sullen corners
    And dazzle us with the blazonry of your sequins,
      Come zipping from the flies,
While all the falling waters sing your praise out of porcelain,
    Come rippling with love, our beautiful grounds for divorce
      With ineluctable thighs,
Our stitch in the side of time. O see, your followers
    Are coming across the patchily-lit, rag-baggedly
      Hunching earth under arches,
Through clumps and bogholes toward you, flying off the handle,
    Rebounding from slumps and falling from the windows of
        wallets,
      Redoubled and vulnerable,
They are coming with the jerks of spastics, with congenital
        hernias
     The multitudinous lovers clutching your outskirts,
      The orphans of your storms,
And bearing their jiggers and bitters, the upright citizens,
    Their faces hanging knock-eyed from their skulls,
      Come floating as proud as punch
To lie at your lofty feet. O whirl us in your drums
    Head over heels together like bingo numbers.
      The show must never go on
Without you, our double-breasted starlet, sweet frump of our days,
    Great punchboard we gloss over and prize open
      Forever and ever.

THE MIDDLE OF NOWHERE

To be here, in the first place, is sufficiently amazing:
The flat, tough, gray-green, prickly, star-shaped weeds
Are the sole proprietors
Of a stretch of clay and shale; the cracks zigzagging
Under bleached husks and stems follow directions
Not yet invented—north
By south, upright by easterly, northwest by nothing—
And a cracked rock the size of a cornerstone
Is the only landmark;
The sun is too high, too rigorous, too downright for measuring.
This patch may have a name and coordinates
By Sextant out of Star
Or out of Map by Compass, but the problem of being
Here is not deducible—though the eyes,
Nose, tongue, and fingers,
The outer and inner ears may suggest some calculations:
With perfect eyesight, a sense of smell, good taste,
A feeling for surfaces,
Judgment of temperature, and absolute pitch, a balancing
Act of a kind may be carried out against
The odds for a moment,
But the curvature of the earth and the curvature of a spine
Have little connection beyond the geotropism
That keeps one round
And the other upright against its natural habit of lying.
Location is the same as dislocation:
The middle of nowhere
Is portable, reusable, and indispensable. It is something
For nothing, the hole in all the assembled data
Through which we look
Beyond the sags and flaps, the lap-overs and interlockings
Of the usual dimensions into the pit
At the heart of our matter,
Which is neither logical nor ecological, abstaining
As it must from left- and right-handedness,
Bilateral judgment,
And all the makers of haphazard dichotomies under the sun.
This is the place where we must be ready to take
The truths or consequences

Of which there are none to be filched or mastered or depended on,
Not even, as it was in the beginning, the Word
Or, here, the squawk of a magpie.

ONE EAR TO THE GROUND

Stretched out on the ground, I hear the news of the night
Pass over and under:
The faraway honks of geese flying blind as stars
 (And hoof- or heartbeats) ,
The squeaks of bats, impaling moths in the air,
Who leave light wings
To flutter by themselves down to the grass
 (And under that grass
The thud and thump of meeting, the weasel's whisper) ,
Through the crackling thorns
Over creekbeds up the ridge and against the moon,
The coyotes howling
All national anthems, cresting, picking up
Where men leave off
 (And, beneath, the rumble of faulted and flawed earth
Shaking its answer) .

WAITING WITH THE SNOWY OWLS

Their yellow eyes as blank as the end
Of winter under the chickenwire,
Nine snowy owls are waiting.

They stand on the ground and stare at anything
Moving, their leg-tufts drifting
Like snow over their talons.

They came south like the snow, when winter hardened
Behind them, to be met by the shots and shouts
Of all our finders and keepers.

Now they wait under the sun for it to melt
What holds them, to run from them or stir
The thawed halves of hearts at their feet.

They stare through the mesh at the green welter
Of spring in the children's zoo. I wait
On the walk beside them, unable to read or write.

TO BE SUNG ON THE WATER

for Rolfe Humphries, 1894–1969

Whatever you say or sing
On the water should be fading.
The air has far to go
After it leaves you,
Rising and falling down
To the sea like the weather.
You needn't sing at all
If, when you hold still,
The wavering of the wind
Against you, against you
Is simpler and more telling.
Listen, and end now
Moved only by the water.

HALCYON DAYS

for James Wright

Remember the day we went to Halcyon
To see the poet? The thick front door was locked
And the door at the top of the stairway, but his door
Had a hole for a doorknob, mesh for a window.
We sat. He smoked a cigar for us, rehearsing
Or reenacting Hell for our benefit—
Two former students who racked their brains for him,
Who went there sober and came away as drunk
As judges, refusing sentence after sentence.

They've taken the place apart, yanked off the roof,
Scrapped all the tubs and beaten the walls out.
The Violent Ward, including the Rec Room,
Has wound up upside down in the driveway
Without permission, and chunks of linoleum
Lie strewn on the slope like manic steppingstones.
They're levelling it and the bluff with a bulldozer,
Smoothing everything out. It's visitors' day
All day and all night from this day forward.
Here lay one whose nest was built on water.

THE SURVIVOR

We found the salmon on its side, the river no longer
Covering all of it, the hooked jaws gaping
And closing around as much sharp air as water.

It lay on the stones, far from the nesting hollow,
Its dark flanks battered cadaver-white, and fungus
Scaling its gills the color of marigolds.

"Help it," she said. "I can't help it, it's dying"—
Looking hard at the upper eye struck dull
As a stone, overcast with cataracts.

But it splashed to life, came scuttering, fishtailing forward
As if the two of us were a place upstream,
And we saw its humpback writhe ashore, then tilt

Upright in an inch of water. It mouthed the ripples
And stared with both eyes now at the empty sunlight,
Not knowing where it was. I turned it away

With my boot, catching my breath. It lurched and slid
To a pool as deep as its body, then lunged in the current
And gradually fell downstream, while we followed it

(Where the yellow leaves came scattering to the shallows)
And watched its dorsal fin be joined by another
To hang there, wavering, for the cold time being.

ONE MORE FOR THE RAIN

The rain is pummelling
Our hemlock again and again,
And slapdash lightning knocks
The daylight out of the sky.
My love, what passes
For air in a cloudburst comes
Through all the baffling branches,
Lifting dust to the light,
To the disembodied wind
And water around us
Like the chaos and old night
We spilled out of these hearts
To make our firmament.

THE BREAK OF DAY

Quivering through the field
Like the stubble of the night,
The first straw-colored light
Touches our windowsill.
Real straw lies in the stable.
Real wheat lies under stone.
Whenever we lie down,
My love, we turn together
Toward the edge of dawn
And fall for the thousandth time
Under the sweeping scythe
That levels all we have
To keep under the sun.

GIFT WRAPPING

Already imagining her
Unwrapping it, I fold the corners,
Putting paper and ribbon between her
And this small box. I could hand it over
Out in the open: why bother to catch her eye
With floss and glitter?
Looking manhandled, it lies there
Like something lost in the mail, the bow
On backwards. And minutes from now,
She will have seen what it is.
But between her guesswork
And the lifting of the lid, I can delay
All disappointments: the give and take
Of love is in the immediate present
Again, though I can't remember myself
What's in it for her.

LAST WORDS OF THE HUMAN FLY

I swear by the bottomless pit of my stomach,
I had no head for heights.
But stairways and elevators
Were meant for sinking fingernail-filing clerks
And rising janitors,
Not for a rank outsider. When the gargoyles vanished
And the caryatids with their lofty bosoms,
I found something else to cling to
In spite of the architects:
Not the snouts of air-conditioners
Or the ankles of swash-buckling window-washers,
But myself: I stick to what I am.
When I let go, I'll break to thousands of eyes.

THE VACATION

The Indian asked me, "How come you're not working?"
He had on jeans and most of a shirt, one shoe and a Stetson.

I said I was on vacation. He picked up the word
And muttered it, trying it on himself. It didn't fit.

"That means you save up in the winter," he said,
"Then spend it?" Yes, I told him it was something like that.

We stood for a minute looking at half of Montana:
A prairie stretching past a jail and a junkyard

Where the sheep and coyotes both get stiff on the weather
Or poisoned baits, where a vulture can't make a living,

And nobody counts much, with or without a treaty.
He said, "I saved up thirty-nine years, that's all I got,

The years. You got to build a vacation like a house,
One brick at a time." I said I didn't doubt it.

"We're supposed to save up summer for the winter,"
He said, "but look at how hot. It bakes the dirt

Like bricks. If I had a brick, I'd drink it."
I gave him the price of a brick, and he took it.

And he went back to work at saving up years
For all the good it would do him. I was no help.

And that was my vacation: I vacated a house
And went to a vacant place palmed off on the Indians

For recreation, in order to recreate, supposedly,
A self worth carrying in this hod on my shoulders.

That end of Montana is still the end of Montana.
This is my work, and this is the end of it.

DO NOT PROCEED BEYOND THIS POINT
WITHOUT A GUIDE

The official warning, nailed to a hemlock,
Doesn't say why. I stand with my back to it,
Afraid I've come as far as I can
By being stubborn, and look
Downward for miles at the hazy crags and spurs.

A rubble-covered ridge like a bombed stairway
Leads up beyond the sign. It doesn't
Seem any worse than what I've climbed already.
Why should I have to take a guide along
To watch me scaring myself to death?

What was it I wanted? A chance to look around
On a high rock already named and numbered
By somebody else? A chance to shout
Over the heads of people who quit sooner?
Shout what? I can't go tell it on the mountain.

I sit for a while, raking the dead leaves
Out of my lungs and travelling light-headed
Downward again in my mind's eye, till there's nothing
Left of my feet but rags and bones
And nothing to look down on but my shoes.

The closer I come to it, the harder it is to doubt
How well this mountain can take me or leave me.
The hemlock had more sense. It stayed where it was,
Grew up and down at the same time, branch and root,
Being a guide instead of needing one.

THE OTHER SIDE OF THE MOUNTAIN

To walk downhill you must lean partially backwards,
Heels digging in,
While your body gets more help than it can use
In following directions—
Because it's possible simply to fall down
The way you're going
Instead of climbing against it. The baffling dead-ends
Of travelling upward
Are turned around now, their openings leading down
To the land you promised
Yourself, beyond box canyons and blind-draws.
They branch repeatedly,
But the direction you choose should be as easy to take
As your right hand.
The sky is a constant; even its variables
Like cirrus and cumulus
Will cancel each other out in a rough balance,
Taking turns at weather.
The wind may bluff and bluster and cut corners
Or skip a whole valley,
But eventually it has nothing to do with you,
Not even when it throws
The dust of your own country in your eyes.
At dawn, at darkness,
The sun will be here or there, full-face, rear-view;
It evens out in the end.
You must keep your goal in mind as clear as day
Though it doesn't matter
What you may think it looks like: second-sight
Is simply perseverance;
And getting there from here is a set of stages
Demanding candle-power,
Foot-pounds and simple levers, thirst and hunger.
Signposts are seasonal
And not forensic: one end may come to a point
And the other be indented,
But the words will be gone, and the rusty earth and air
Will have eaten the pole and nails.
You must take time to notice what grows on rocks
Or squeezes between them—

The gnawing lichen, bone-weed and thorny scrub—
All hanging tough
And gnarling for elbow room or squatters' rights.
These are the straighteners,
The levellers at work on the thick and crooked:
Some distant species
Will find the world made flat by the likes of these.
You must do your bit
By scuffing downhill heel-first on behalf of erosion,
For the sake of another time
When the mountains are made plain and anyone standing
Can see from here to there
Without half-trying. When your shoes are out of step
And your clothes are a burden
And you feel bone-tired, sit down and look around.
You're there. No matter what
You had in mind as a proper circumstance,
You've come to it at last:
A rock-strewn slope from which you have a view
Of a further rock-strewn slope.
You can pick up dust in your hand and let it fall.
The place is real.
You can bite a grass-stem, look, take a deep breath
And, naturally, let it go.

DOING TIME

Do your own time, say prisoners
To those who spill their lives to others.
I serve my indeterminate years
Through these concurrent sentences
Out of a hope to get time off
For good behavior, doing life
For willful failure to report
On what goes on and on in the heart.

THE FIRST LAW OF MOTION

"Every body perseveres in its state of rest, or of uniform
motion in a right line, unless it is compelled to change that
state by forces impressed thereon."
—Isaac Newton, *Principia Mathematica*

Staying strictly in line and going
Along with a gag or swinging
Far out and back or simply wheeling
Into the home-stretch again and again,
Not shoving or stalling, but coasting
And playing it smooth, pretending
To make light of it, you can seem
To be keeping it up forever, needing
Little or nothing but your own
Dead weight to meet
The demands of momentum,
But there's no way out of touching
Something or being touched, and like it
Or not, you're going to be
Slowing down because turning
A corner means coming to a dead
Halt, however slight, to change direction,
And your impulse to get moving
Again may never move you, so keeping time
Is as inhuman as the strict first law
Of motion, and going off on your own
On some lopsided jagged course
For which there's no equation, some unbecoming
Switchbacked crossfooted trek in a maze
Of your own invention, some dying
Fall no star could fix, is a state of being
Human at least, and so, at last, is stopping.

THE FLOATING LADY

The Professor sawed her in half and put her back
Together; chopped off her head, restored it; sat her
Down in a box and thrust long dozens of swords
Through where she was, then brought her out unharmed.
And now he waves her into a final trance
And rests her on a table under a sheet
As white as any lady in a morgue.
She rises smoothly into the spotlit air
And hovers there to music, floating on nothing.

He stands underneath, commanding her to move
Sideways or forward, and she does. He slides
A hoop around her. Isn't she beautiful
Under the sheet where none of us can see her?
Here in the balcony, floating even higher
Than she, we put ourselves in her position,
Lying beside her, trying to weigh her down
To a world of unsliced bodies and mattresses
Where we might love her heavily forever.

But now the Professor yanks the cloth away,
And she's gone. She has disappeared like all her wounds
From crosscut saw and guillotine and sword
And doesn't come back. The Professor takes applause
Like a man saying Q.E.D. to a piece of logic
On a bare stage with the empty sheet in his arms.

THE MAKERS OF RAIN

We sit at the top of the Pyramid of the Magician
Our last day in Uxmal, afraid
Of the sheer steps and the ranks of the rain gods,
The rows of Chacmuls in stone with their high-flung,
    fanfaring noses.
Having guided ourselves this far, we look
At the ruined ball-court and, beyond, the iguanas basking
In the cracked fretwork of the Palace of the Governor,
The stone jaguars mating in the plaza
By the broken phallus, and with its jammed perspective,
    the quadrangle
Where four classes of priests took charge of the rain.

Not even the Governors were allowed this high to lord it
Over the land from the mouth of the temple
Whose intricate façade is a Chacmul's face
Behind our backs. Not daring to ask for a change in the deep sky,
We wait for our lives to topple
Like the rest, though our hands hold us together, balancing
Our love against the weight of evidence
That has caved in one whole side of this pyramid.

We are masters of nothing we survey,
But what the Magician did from here—chant with his arms
    outstretched
Over a dying city or reach halfway to the clouds sailing aloof
Over the maize fields—is ours to try, since we believe in magic,
Believe we can climb to it slowly, being frightened,
That it can break suddenly out of stone or out of the dry air.
As priest and priestess of ourselves, before praying for rain,
We weep to show it how.

THE DOVES OF MÉRIDA

We took ourselves to market in Mérida,
Shopping and being shopped
Under the iron roof where, steaming like frijoles,
We were caught up short
After the hammocks and sandals in the long aisles
To find our eyes full of birds:
They sat in cages, jammed in each other's rafters,
The cardinals and honey creepers,
The grackles and finches—and there lay the mourning doves
Huddled together,
Their powdery-rose and mother-of-pearl necks
Twisting out of fear.
Ten pesos per dove, said the *hombre de rapiña,*
The only bargainer
In all of the Yucatan who wouldn't bargain:
A fixed corona of silver
For each, as sure as the price of a medal in the Cathedral
Or a bottle of clear water.
We carried five in a cage through the choking streets,
Dos gringos locos,
And plied them with cracked heads of the god of maize,
With water in ashtrays
On the terrace of the hotel. They ate and drank,
Watching life sideways
In the sunlight shrinking back to the Gulf's belly.
We opened their door
And hoped for peace, for land after the flood,
Or hoped for hope.

The first one flew with matted, rump-sprung tailfeathers
High among shade trees
To hold all night in the wind from Cozumel,
To wait for sunrise
And the school of his masters in the Plaza de la Independencia:
The lean gray city pigeons.
The second flew two walls and houses away
To land among turkeys
And chickens as small as he in the rock-strewn courtyard
To peck, in order, at dirt
And fatten himself as a squab for his destiny.

The third one rose
As high as the green caryatids at the roof of the Palacio
De Avis Rent-a-Car,
Then fell to be done to a turn in the sunny gutter,
Drawing the vultures down
In the morning to break their fast. And the fourth,
Heart-forward and swift,
Flew past the tortoiseshell shop of Sr. Carrillo Gonzalez
Where the stuffed turtles
Pluck their guitars in rows as if mourning their shells,
Over vendors wearing skulls
And over the barking dogs in the butcher's attic
And the zippered armadillos,
Not touching the broken glass on the tops of the walls
Around the dense gardens
Of the descendants of Don Francisco de Montejo—the Conqueror,
The dismantler of the gods—
As sweet and close as pyramids of fruit salad.
It skimmed past the zoo
And the *barrios* where adobe, heaped up like sandbags,
Looked something like houses,
And past the Aeropuerto, high over the highway
And the heaped-up burros
Where the thatched huts crackle and shrink in the day's oven
And the children shrink from the doors
And the stucco drops from the empty bell-towers of churches,
Flew over gigantic rows
Of sisal patched against jungle rooted in ruins,
Past the rubble of cities
And over the iguanas shaking their fringed jowls
At the last of the light,
And flew before dark to the gray-green hummocks of Uxmal
Past the steep empty stairs
Of the Pyramid of the Magician. At the broken Casa de las
    Palomas
It flapped to its rest
Where the Mayans left holes in stone for the singing wind,
The maker of doves and rain.

And the fifth one circled upward, groping for distance,
Turning half gold,
And disappeared before our eyes could tell it apart
From what was beyond it.

We gave the empty cage, for what it was worth,
To a straight-faced waiter,
Then flew away, flew far in the dead of night
To our own fortunes.

THE GATHERING OF THE LOONS

In the dead calm before darkness near the shore
The loons are gathering, rippling blue-gray
As slow as driftwood, the lighthouse blinking
And sweeping across the long calls of the gulls,
The scoters darkening, the breathlessly sighing
Wingbeats of goldeneyes across the marshgrass
Lifting the widgeons up in gold-streaked wedges
To take one way toward night against the mountains,
And the still loons, the solitary loons
Drifting together out into the bay,
The silent loons all floating toward sleep.

OLD MAN, OLD MAN

Young men, not knowing what to remember,
Come to this hiding place of the moons and years,
To this Old Man. Old Man, they say, where should we go?
Where did you find what you remember? Was it perched
    in a tree?
Did it hover deep in the white water? Was it covered over
With dead stalks in the grass? Will we taste it
If our mouths have long lain empty?
Will we feel it between our eyes if we face the wind
All night, and turn the color of earth?
If we lie down in the rain, can we remember sunlight?

He answers, I have become the best and worst I dreamed.
When I move my feet, the ground moves under them.
When I lie down, I fit the earth too well.
Stones long under water will burst in the fire, but stones
Long in the sun and under the dry night
Will ring when you strike them. Or break in two.
There were always many places to beg for answers:
Now the places themselves have come in close to be told.
I have called even my voice in close to whisper with it:
Every secret is as near as your fingers.
If your heart stutters with pain and hope,
Bend forward over it like a man at a small campfire.

LOST

Stand still. The trees ahead and bushes beside you
Are not lost. Wherever you are is called Here,
And you must treat it as a powerful stranger,
Must ask permission to know it and be known.
The forest breathes. Listen. It answers,
I have made this place around you.
If you leave it, you may come back again, saying Here.
No two trees are the same to Raven.
No two branches are the same to Wren.
If what a tree or a bush does is lost on you,
You are surely lost. Stand still. The forest knows
Where you are. You must let it find you.

FOG

Though your brothers, after the long hunt and the fasting,
After holding still, have found Fox, Bear Mother,
Or Snake at their sides and taken them
Into the empty mouths of their spirits,
Do not be jealous. They will be cunning
Or strong or good at dreaming. Do not be ashamed
That you—when the day changed, when the first hour
Came falling suddenly over the last hour—
Found only Fog as eye of your heart opened.

Now when your feet touch earth, nothing will know you.
You will move without moving a leaf,
Climb the steep cliffside as easily as Hawk,
Cross water, pass silently as Owl.
You will become trees by holding them inside you,
And tall stones, become a whole valley
Where birds fall still, where men stay close to fires.
You without wings or hands will gleam against them,
They will breathe you, they will be lost in you,
Your song will be the silence between their songs,
Your white darkness will teach them,
You will wrap all love and fear in a beautiful blindness.

from
SLEEPING IN THE WOODS
(1974)

THE SINGING LESSON

You must stand erect but at your ease, a posture
Demanding a compromise
Between your spine and your head, your best face forward,
Your willful hands
Not beckoning or clenching or sweeping upward
But drawn in close:
A man with his arms spread wide is asking for it,
A martyred beggar,
A flightless bird on the nest dreaming of flying.
For your full resonance
You must keep your inspiring and expiring moments
Divided but equal,
Not locked like antagonists from breast to throat,
Choking toward silence.

If you have learned, with labor and luck, the measures
You were meant to complete,
You may find yourself before an audience
Singing into the light,
Transforming the air you breathe—that malleable wreckage,
That graveyard of shouts,
That inexhaustible pool of chatter and whimpers—
Into deathless music.
But remember, with your mouth wide open, eyes shut,
Some men will wonder,
When they look at you without listening, whether
You're singing or dying.
Take care to be heard. But even singing alone,
Singing for nothing,
Singing to empty space in no one's honor,
Keep time: it will tell
When you must give the final end-stopped movement
Your tacit approval.

BEGINNING

By the stiff sheaves of ferns
And moss like green hoarfrost
I waded upstream on stones
The shades of ice
On a day when the half-frozen
Rain fell over rain
Through the lashed hemlocks
And the red roots of cedars streamed
Downstream, colder than nerves.
Not even winter wrens
Or dippers with sheathing eyelids
Had come to this:
The water plunged at its work
From slab to slab, alone,
Into pools moss-dark at noon.
I came to a stand of alders
As pale as my bones
And waited a dead hour
In the thawing dirt at their roots
Like them to begin again.

THE BAD FISHERMAN

At first, I thought my heart was in it: trembling on the shore,
I cast my spinner over the green current
And felt it bump downstream on the stones, my throat pulsing
Like a cormorant's. As sure as I was standing in water,
I would take the father of all fish out of the river.

Some I hadn't dreamed I could see leaping
Again and again at the head of a long drift—
A summer run of steelhead or blackmouth salmon
Landing as loud as children diving, hazel-gray bellies
Arching beyond the reach of my line.

I'd have beginner's luck: I was sure of it,
Putting up with the unaccustomed homework
Of dropper loops and clinch knots, of threading snap-swivels
Or tracing a spidery maze of nylon back through willows
To find where I'd caught myself

Or fighting to free my lure from the low branches
After a haywire backswing. It rained, it stopped, a haze
Came out of the woods at sundown
To drink at the river, a hatch of caddis-flies
Flew downwind into the mouths of other cutthroats.

And still I kept casting and casting away,
Imagining the great trout that would lash at my hook
And put me to the spinning and thrashing labor of landing it
While we gaped at each other's terrible elements
At last after my years of barely touching the surface.

I went home in the dark with nothing,
But kept on fishing, not knowing what I'd learned
That first day out of natural clumsiness
With my shadow all over the water, my loud voice swearing,
And the unknown fish breaking beyond me.

Since then, I've held them in my hands and stared
Into that round incredulous eye gone flat, glazed over
With death, the lucid death I'd nearly forgotten

While casting around for want of something better,
And felt their sparse, cold blood warming my fingers.

I've gutted my last rainbow.
Instead, I wait and watch at the river's edge,
Sometime for hours, empty handed,
As still as a heron, wishing for its eye
To see, only to see through the water.

TALKING TO BARR CREEK

Under the peachleaf willows, alders, and choke cherries,
By coltsfoot, devil's club, sweet-after-death,
And bittersweet nightshade,
Like a fool, I sit here talking to you, begging a favor,
A lesson as hard and long as your bed of stones
To hold me together.
At first, thinking of you, my mind slid down like a leaf
From source to mouth, as if you were only one
Piece of yourself at a time,
As if you were nowhere but here or there, nothing but now,
One place, one measure. But you are all at once,
Beginning through ending.
What man could look at you all day and not be a beggar?
How could he take his eyes at their face-value?
How could his body
Bear its dead weight? Grant me your endless, ungrudging impulse
Forward, the lavishness of your light movements,
Your constant inconstancy,
Your leaping and shallowing, your stretches of black and amber,
Bluing and whitening, your long-drawn wearing away,
Your sudden stillness.
From the mountain lake ten miles uphill to the broad river,
Teach me your spirit, going yet staying, being
Born, vanishing, enduring.

THE FIRST PLACE

For a mile by green-and-gold light, wading upstream,
Uncertain of our feet in the rush and shimmer
Among the touching ferns, by our touching fingers,
And led by wren-song through alders felled by beavers,
We came to a pool flowing deep
And swift below water-striders, where shelving moss
Gave way at last to our bodies on the shore.

Then, while the rainbows leaped, she opened
The gift of her nakedness, stepped into that stream,
Into water so cold my hand lay nearly frozen
In the rippling shallows, so cold it seemed
Already ice to hold us apart forever.

But she was singing, welcoming the wonder
Of the river that held her light as her beauty,
And streaming with light, with the sun swept down
Through cedar and hemlock, we saw the beginning
As our eyes met over the water. She came ashore,
And we put our lives in our hands on a morning
That had no ending.

Yet suddenly I went plunging in without her
And felt the cold touching its blood brother:
That other cold held back in the heart's shadow
Against the day when it must fight
What it most fears: love's burning entrance. The shock
Blunted my hands and feet and threw me sidelong
In a circling eddy, buffeted by streamers
Bounding over the deeper stones, going white
As my skin while I flailed, faltered inshore
To a sandbar, numb as a half-man.

She waded toward me out of mercy
For a half-frozen lover, and we swam together
Easily as the down-winding current
Drawn from us like our breath
Till under our very eyelids, through our fingers,
Not alone, the river said, *not alone*
(Though chilling us deep as our swaying backbones),

And the small terrible fish in our bloodstreams,
In the veins of our minds' eyes, vanished
Upstream to spawn in the last place on earth
We could have hoped for: the first place.

THE VOW

By the snowy owl in the fog
And the skate's egg and the toad
That sang once in our room
And the sturgeon's head and the scoter
Asleep on the shore and the sow
Snoring beyond her dugs,
By the dazed newborn lamb,
By the mockingbird and the doves
Turned out of their cages,
By herons and star-nosed moles,
By the muzzles of burros
And the young quail in your palm,
By the one-legged kinglet, the hawk
Stooped at our singing rosebush,
By the lark, by the dying turkey,
By the goats dancing for hens,
By the harbor seal beyond us
And the salmon at our feet,
I set my hand to love.

SLOW COUNTRY

When you come to slow country, you will move
In the steady company
Of your hands and feet, your breath as still as a pool.
The landscape around you
Will seem as fixed as a permanent kingdom
Where the shape of the wind
Can not be found in any cloud or tree.
If your hand goes out
To a weed or a grassblade, you will have hours to spare
To wonder how it has come to be
 (Before your fingers break it) that you have nothing
Of yours to reach as deeply
Between the stones. If your watch falls from your hand,
It will not break
Until it has taken time to strike the ground;
Meanwhile, you may follow it
And feel as detached as a true lord of the land
When it shatters in glassy splendor:
You will measure everything equally well thereafter.
Even spilled water
Will seem as placid and ornate as ice.
All your dear enemies,
Both real and imagined, will wait in their hiding places,
Waver, then float toward you,
More and more clearly known by sun- and moonlight;
They will never reach you
Except as shrinking familiars, ripe with age.
It will seem useless
To shout in the prolonged air, since you will notice
Even a scream has a beginning,
An expansive middle, and a hapless ending
Around which the silence
Has grown more calm than ever. Between your lips
And your tongue, a sweetness;
Between your lurching heart and your wits, a passage.
Stay there. You will have time
Between the dream of embracing and the full embrace
To find your love
Lying beneath you like the willing earth,
Neither turning nor falling.

TO BE WRITTEN IN BRAILLE

This is not for our eyes:
They may wander, restless,
Too far from us,
Led astray by shadows.

This is not for our ears:
We are poor listeners
In that strange distress
Following all whispers.

But for our fingers:
Love, touch these silent arbors
And their dark flowers.
All of them are yours.

SONG FOR THE WORST DAY

It has come shambling
Out of the mountains, the unwelcome daylight,
The ravenous morning.
What can it do but gnaw us both to the bone
By the red of evening?
Love, sing to survive this stripping away,
This terrible searching.
Sing something to be left in the long night,
To bring to nothing.

LIVING IN THE RUINS

The tyranny of doors swung shut and bolted
Against a knock or the scratching darkness
Has ended with these breaks in your walls
Where anything may leave or enter
As the moon and the wind decide. The ceiling
Has settled comfortably across the floor;
The stairways have faltered
Like waterfalls whose careless water
Is falling as far as all split-level living
To its logical conclusion in rubble.

Lean at a window now and feel no longing
For all that lay out of reach: it will reach you
Simply, uncalled-for, here in this open season,
And you must take what comes to your windowsill
To make itself at home, while broken glass
Blooms where the iris was.

What happens naturally is the advent of moss
Turning these stones to sand, establishing
The separation of powers with its rootless searching.
You have nothing to be coveted but your life:
Tending a fire to make your share of the weather
And living in these ruins to reconnoitre
Your strangest neighbor: night falling around you.

MOVING INTO THE GARDEN

Moving into the garden, we settle down
Between the birdbath and the hollyhocks
To wait for the beginning, leaving behind
The house we served for the best years of its life,
Making ourselves at home by the grass spider's
Hollow-throated nest in the ivy.

We have much to learn, such as what to do all day
In the rain that leans the roses against us
And how to follow all night the important paths
Of snails and shy leaf-rollers and lace bugs
And what to make of ourselves among them
At dawn when the cold light touches our fingers

That are no longer thinking of uprooting
Or pruning or transplanting but following
This fall the columbine and bleeding heart
Darkening together, the maidenhair
Closing away like all perennials,
Hardy or delicate, and turning under.

We lift handfuls of earth (is it motherly
Now? was it once? will it be again?)
And wait for the brambles to rise over the slope
Beside us like slow green breakers striking a seawall
To join with us, to mingle with what we love,
With what we've gathered here against the winter.

AN OFFERING FOR DUNGENESS BAY

1

The tern, his lean, slant wings
Swivelling, lifts and hovers
Over the glassy bay,
Then plunges suddenly into that breaking mirror,
Into himself, and rises, bearing silver
In his beak and trailing silver
Falling to meet itself over and over.

2

Over the slow surf
Where the moon is opening,
Begin, the plover cries,
And beyond the shallows
The far-off answer,
Again, again, again,
Under the white wind
And the long boom of the breakers
Where the still whiter branches
Lie pitched and planted deep,
Only begin, the water says,
And the rest will follow.

3

Dusk and low tide and the sanderlings
Alighting in their hundreds by the last of the light
On seawrack floating in the final ripples
Lightly, scarcely touching, and now telling
This night, *Here,* and this night coming,
Here, where we are, as their beaks turn down and thin,
As fine as sandgrains, *Here is the place.*

4

The geese at the brim of darkness are beginning
To rise from the bay, a few at first in formless
Clusters low to the water, their black wings beating
And whistling like shorebirds to bear them up, and calling
To others, to others as they circle wider

Over the shelving cove, and now they gather
High toward the marsh in chevrons and echelons,
Merging and interweaving, their long necks turning
Seaward and upward, catching a wash of moonlight
And rising further and further, stretching away,
Lifting, beginning again, going on and on.

MUSE

Cackling, smelling of camphor, crumbs of pink icing
Clinging to her lips, her lipstick smeared
Halfway around her neck, her cracked teeth bristling
With bloody splinters, she leans over my shoulder.
Oh my only hope, my lost dumfounding baggage,
My gristle-breasted, slack-jawed zealot, kiss me again.

THE LABORS OF THOR

Stiff as the icicles in their beards, the Ice Kings
Sat in the great cold hall and stared at Thor
Who had lumbered this far north to stagger them
With his gifts, which (back at home) seemed scarcely human.

"Immodesty forbids," his sideman Loki
Proclaimed throughout the preliminary bragging
And reeled off Thor's accomplishments, fit for Sagas
Or a seat on the bench of the gods. With a sliver of beard

An Ice King picked his teeth: "Is he a drinker?"
And Loki boasted of challengers laid out
As cold as pickled herring. The Ice King offered
A horn-cup long as a harp's neck, full of mead.

Thor braced himself for elbow and belly room
And tipped the cup and drank as deep as mackerel,
Then deeper, reaching down for the halibut
Till his broad belt buckled. He had quaffed one inch.

"Maybe he's better at something else," an Ice King
Muttered, yawning. Remembering the boulders
He'd seen Thor heave and toss in the pitch of anger,
Loki proposed a bout of lifting weights.

"You men have been humping rocks from here to there
For ages," an Ice King said. "They cut no ice.
Lift something harder." And he whistled out
A gray-green cat with cold, mouseholey eyes.

Thor gave it a pat, then thrust both heavy hands
Under it, stooped and heisted, heisted again,
Turned red in the face and bit his lip and heisted
From the bottom of his heart—and lifted one limp forepaw.

Now pink in the face himself, Loki said quickly
That heroes can have bad days, like bards and beggars,
But Thor of all mortals was the grossest wrestler
And would stake his demigodhood on one fall.

Seeming too bored to bother, an Ice King waved
His chilly fingers around the mead-hall, saying,
"Does anyone need some trifling exercise
Before we go glacier-calving in the morning?"

An old crone hobbled in, foul-faced and gamy,
As bent in the back as any bitch of burden,
As gray as water, as feeble as an oyster.
An Ice King said, "She's thrown some boys in her time."

Thor would have left, insulted, but Loki whispered,
"When the word gets south, she'll be at least an ogress."
Thor reached out sullenly and grabbed her elbow,
But she quicksilvered him and grinned her gums.

Thor tried his patented hammerlock takedown,
But she melted away like steam from a leaky sauna.
He tried a whole Nelson: it shrank to half, to a quarter,
Then nothing. He stood there, panting at the ceiling,

"Who got me into this demigoddiness?"
As flashy as lightning, the woman belted him
With her bony fist and boomed him to one knee,
But fell to a knee herself, as pale as moonlight.

Bawling for shame, Thor left by the back door,
Refusing to be consoled by Loki's plans
For a quick revision of the Northodox Version
Of the evening's deeds, including Thor's translation

From vulnerable flesh and sinew into a dish
Fit for the gods and a full apotheosis
With catches and special effects by the sharpest gleemen
Available in an otherwise flat season.

He went back south, tasting his bitter lesson
Moment by moment for the rest of his life,
Believing himself a pushover faking greatness
Along a tawdry strain of misadventures.

Meanwhile, the Ice Kings trembled in their chairs
But not from the cold: they'd seen a man hoist high
The Great Horn-Cup that ends deep in the ocean
And lower all Seven Seas by his own stature;

They'd seen him budge the Cat of the World and heft
The pillar of one paw, the whole north corner;
They'd seen a mere man wrestle with Death herself
And match her knee for knee, grunting like thunder.

BEAUTY AND THE BEAST

Men wept when they saw her breasts, squinted with pain
At her clear profile, boggled at her knees,
Turned slack-jawed at her rear-view walking away,
And every available inch of her hair and skin
Had been touched by love poems and delicious gossip.
The most jaundiced and jaded people in the village
Agreed with the Prince: young Beauty was a beauty.

But through the long day he doused and plucked his roses,
Drained and refilled his moat, or caulked his dungeons,
And all night long he clocked the erring planets,
Pondered the lives of saints like a Latin-monger,
Or sat up half-seas over with sick falcons,
While Beauty lingered in her sheerest nightgowns
With the light behind her, wilting from sheer boredom.

"You're a bore!" she said. "Prince Charming is a bore!"
She cried to the gaping seamstresses and fishwives.
"He's a bore!" she yelled to the scullions and butcher's helpers.
"That's tedious, bland, preoccupied, prickling Princeling
Is a bore's bore!" she told the bloody barbers
And waxy chandlers leaning out to watch her
Dragging her rear-view home to Mother and Father.

But deep in the woods, behind a bush, the Beast
Had big ideas about her. When she slipped by,
Hiking her skirts to give her legs free sway
And trailing a lovely, savage, faint aroma
Fit to unman a beast, the Beast said, "Beauty,
Come live with me in the bushes where it's chancy,
Where it's scare and scare alike, where it's quick and murky."

She looked him over. Though the light was patchy,
She could see him better than she wanted to:
Wherever men have skin, the Beast had hair;
Wherever men have hair, he had black bristles;
Wherever men have bristles, he grew teeth;
And wherever men have teeth, his snaggling tusks
Lapped over his smile. So Beauty said, "No thank you."

"You'd be a sweet relief. I'd gorge on you.
I'm sick of retching my time with hags and gorgons.
You're gorgeous. Put down my rising gorge forever."
She remembered her mother whispering: *The Beast
Is a bargain. It's a well-known fact that, later,
He turns into a Prince, humble and handsome,
With unlimited credit and your father's mustache.*

*So all you have to do is grin and bear him
Till the worst is over.* But Beauty felt uncertain.
Still, after the Prince, it seemed like now or never,
And maybe all men were monsters when they saw her,
And maybe the ugliest would teach her sooner.
Her heart felt colder than a wizard's whistle:
She said, "You Beast, how can I say I love you?"

With horny fingers caressing everything
Available on the little world of her body,
The Beast then took her gently, his rich odor
Wafting about them like the mist from graveyards,
And Beauty began to branch out like a castle
Taller than trees, and from the highest tower
She loosened her long hair, and the Beast climbed it.

When he was spent, he lay beside her, brushing
Leaves from her buttresses, and said, "I love you."
She shrank back to herself and felt afraid.
"You'll change into something much more comfortable
Now that you've taken me," she said. "I know:
You'll be transformed to someone like Prince Charming."
"I'm always like this," he said, and drooled a little.

"If you're going to change, change now," she told him,
        weeping.
"Peel off that monster suit and get it over."
"I wear myself out, not in," he said. "I'll love you
In all the worst ways, as clumsily as heaven."
"Thank God," she said. And Beauty and the Beast
Stole off together, arm in hairy arm,
And made themselves scarce in the bewitching forest.

UNLOADING THE ELEPHANTS

Out of the sliding doors
Of steel-gray boxcars
The trunks come groping
Through the gray morning.
Where are we now?
The greatest show
Is on earth, trumpeting
Down the steep ramps and bracing
Forelegs against the heavy
Heavenly bodies
They so carefully balance
Like the commandments
Shouted to massive heads, to ears
Pondering old orders,
Older than canvas.
Why are you keeping us?
In a huge row, seventeen
Elephants. *Why must we learn
From you? What have we done
To be so weighted down?*
Trunks raised, they shuffle forward
To the long parade.

SNAKE HUNT

On sloping, shattered granite, the snake man
From the zoo bent over the half-shaded crannies
Where rattlesnakes take turns out of the sun,
Stared hard, nodded at me, then lunged
With his thick gloves and yanked one up like a root.

And the whole hillside sprang to death with a hissing
Metallic chattering rattle: they came out writhing
In his fists, uncoiling from daydreams,
Pale bellies looping out of darker diamonds
In the shredded sunlight, dropping into his sack.

As I knelt on rocks, my blood went cold as theirs.
One snake coughed up a mouse. I saw what a mouse
Knows, as well as anyone: there, beside me,
In a cleft a foot away from my braced fingers,
Still in its coils, a rattler stirred from sleep.

It moved the wedge of its head back into shadow
And stared at me, harder than I could answer,
Till the gloves came down between us. In the sack,
Like the disembodied muscles of a torso,
It and the others searched among themselves

For the lost good place. I saw them later
Behind plate-glass, wearing their last skins.
They held their venom behind wide-open eyes.

WORMS

When the spade turns over, the worms
In their sheared gangways, turning tail, go thin
Among clods or blunt out in the open,
Half-hitching in fishermen's knots and flinching
At sunlight, the pulsing line of their hearts
Strung out to be abandoned, sinking backward
And forward among the roots, like them,
Like elvers in seaweed, mouthing the darkness,
All taken in by the darkness of their mouths.

AT THE HEMINGWAY MEMORIAL

Ketchum, Idaho

The day's bone dry. I've come through Sun Valley
To sit beside your rock and your greening bust
Above the Big Lost River
Where sage and bitterbush and broom
Have held their own, where the cicadas
Chirr through the cottonwoods in the dead of summer.

The plaque says you're a part of this forever,
Especially the "high blue windless skies" of the Sawtooths,
And looking at big lost Papa's place,
I believe it. The road's as hard,
As shimmering, straight, and spare as early you.
The style is still the man when it deserts him:

By my foot, the husk of a cicada nymph
Lies pale as straw—the nervelessly crouched legs,
The head hunched forward hunting for some way out,
The claws grown stiff defending the clenched hollow,
The back split open,
And nothing but nothing to be brave about.

TACHYCARDIA
AT THE FOOT OF THE FIFTH GREEN

My heart is flapping away from me
As I sprawl, pushing down daisies in the fairway,
At the lambing end of March, my chin
And my lips gone numb as the sunshine.

Because I have no one here (or is it *nothing?*)
To put in charge of my breath, I struggle
Not to pass out, afraid of finding myself
Unable to dream for a last time,

Or, as now, for the first time since I was two,
Unable to stand up for fear of falling.
The next threesome or twosome will see me lying
One on a short par-four and wonder

Whether some crazy or escaping lover
Has given up the serious part of his game
To bed down by a sandtrap, keeping his eye on clouds
Instead of the ball or the flag.

Will I seem just a temporary hazard
Like casual water, to be played around?
Frogs croak. A red-tailed hawk
And a marsh hawk have flown by, bearing their names.

I hear a white-crowned sparrow's brilliant announcement,
But then some warbler, nameless, exasperating,
Reminds me how little I recognize
With or without my wits, how dimly I listen.

If my body's guest isn't thrown off the course
For this unplayable lie, I'll live to learn
What species each of us is. My ball nestles beside me
Inert and unlikely, like a marble egg.

ELEGY FOR A WOMAN
WHO REMEMBERED EVERYTHING

She knew the grades of all her neighbors' children, the birthdays
Of cousins once removed, the addresses of friends who had moved
Once at least—to the coordinates of cemeteries
Where their choice views lay over their front feet.

If it had a name or a number, she missed nothing:
A mailman's neck size, the unpronounceable village where the
        dentist's
Wife's half-sister ruined her kneecap, an almanac of sutures,
The ingredients of five thousand immemorial crocks.

Her ears were as perfectly pitched as a piano-tuner's.
In the maze of total recall, she met with amazement
The data of each new day, absorbed the absorbing facts and
        the absorbent
Fictions of everyone's life but her own, losing the thread

Of that thin tracery in dialogue hauled back verbatim
Through years leaning cracked and crooked against each other.
Death, you may dictate as rapidly or incoherently as you wish:
She will remember everything about you. Nothing will escape her.

THE MAN WHO SPILLED LIGHT

The man who spilled light wasn't to blame for it.
He was in a hurry to bring it home to the city
Where, everyone said, there was too much darkness:
"Look at those shadows," they said. "They're dangerous.
Who's there? What's that?" and crouching, "Who are *you?*"
So he went and scraped up all the light he could find.

But it was too much to handle and started spilling:
Flakes and star-marks, shafts of it splitting
To ring-light and light gone slack or jagged,
Clouds folded inside out, whole pools
And hummocks and domes of light,
Egg-light, light tied in knots or peeled in swatches,
Daylight as jumbled as jackstraws falling.

Then everything seemed perfectly obvious
Wherever they looked. There was nothing they couldn't see.
The corners and alleys all looked empty,
And no one could think of anything terrible
Except behind their backs, so they all lined up
With their backs to walls and felt perfectly fine.
And the man who'd spilled it felt fine for a while,
But then he noticed people squinting.

They should have been looking at everything, and everything
Should have been perfectly clear, and everyone
Should have seemed perfectly brilliant, there was so much
Dazzle: people were dazzled, they were dazzling,
But they were squinting, trying to make darkness
All over again in the cracks between their eyelids.
So he swept up all the broken light
For pity's sake and put it back where it came from.

ELEGY FOR YARDS, POUNDS, AND GALLONS

A duly concocted body of our elders
Is turning you out of office and schoolroom
Through ten long years, is phasing you
Out of our mouths and lives forever.

Words have been lost before: some hounded
Nearly to death, and some transplanted
With roots dead set against stone,
And some let slide into obscure senescence,

Some even murdered beyond recall like extinct animals—
(It would be cruel to rehearse their names:
They might stir from sleep on the dusty shelves
In pain for a moment).

Yet you, old emblems of distance and heaviness,
Solid and liquid companions, our good measures,
When have so many been forced to languish
For years through a deliberate deathwatch?

How can we name your colorless replacements
Or let them tell us for our time being
How much we weigh, how short we are,
Or how little we have left to drink?

Goodbye to Pounds by the Ton and all their Ounces,
To Gallons, Quarts, and Pints,
To Yards whose Feet are inching their last Mile,
Weighed down, poured out, written off,

And drifting slowly away from us
Like drams, like chains and gills,
To become as quaint as leagues and palms
In an old poem.

NOTE TO A LITERARY CLUB

RACINE—The Middleport Literary Club met Wednesday afternoon at the country home of Mrs. Thereon Johnson near Racine. Mrs. Roy Cassell reviewed a book of poetry titled "Riverbed" by David Wagoner. Mrs. Cassell read excerpts from the volume . . . that displayed the simplicity of his poetry.

—Athens (Ohio) *Messenger*
April 30, 1973

When ladies read poems in the heart of Ohio
On April afternoons under heady trellises,
They see them clearly, simply,
And naturally, having been born there, I did too,
Displaying signs of simplicity even at age five
By reciting a poem (taught me by a well-meaning lady)
Beside a red-plush Presbyterian pulpit
About a bog and a bullfrog
And a grumpy boy on a bumpy log
Learning to say *Cheer-up, cheer-up.*
It all seemed plain and painless to me then,
But now, when I know even more frog-songs by heart,
I try to honor those masters of emphatic repetition
In still more simple ways.

Ladies, cheer up. How can you and I go wrong
Gathering once more by any riverbed
Where something as good as frogs has been known to happen
Once in a great while? I thank you kindly
For your kind of attention. But a word of caution:
I know five poets who escaped from Ohio
And five more who went there on purpose, intending to spawn.
You may be hearing them croak at any moment.

THE BOY OF THE HOUSE

Mother, this morning when I woke
My head stayed undercover.
It didn't get up when I got up.
It said the game was over.

It said if I had to wash a face
To go scout up another
And knife-and-fork a different mouth.
Mother, what's the matter?

The dog hides under the leaky sink.
The cat has swiped its tongue.
What do they know that I don't know?
I think there's something wrong.

The milk has turned. The vacuum bag
Is full of long white hairs,
And what perks up in the coffeepot
Has been dripping down for years.

And what comes out of the picture tube
Is spilling on the carpet.
It's spreading over Father's shoes
As thick as rainbow sherbet.

He's blinking one of his eyes again
Sixty times a minute.
His hands are locked below his chin.
His chin has relish on it.

His toes are aiming left and right.
His nose is pointing up.
Mother, I hear his stomach growl
Like a watchdog at a pup.

Go look behind his socks and shorts,
Borrowed, old, and blue.
You'll find a book with a broken back:
What Every Boy Should Know.

The freezer growls in its gamy room,
Guarding parts of cows,
And through the pounding door I see
Jehovah's Witnesses.

Mother, before I spoil myself,
I'm going back to bed.
I don't mind losing at playing house,
But I mustn't lose my head.

Whoever let me out last night
Forgot to punch my ticket.
My head butts into my pillow now
Like a ram into a thicket.

LITANY

Our Sister of the Disposable Dolls and Doilies
    (Who was a bride and might have danced again),
        Remember us among your souvenir pillows
           At the hearth of your heart beside the broken
                wishbones.
Our Brother of Safety Glass and Belted Nylons
    (Who was a groom and should have served again),
        Enlarge us in glossies, bear our black-and-whiteness
        By the bridges, lifts, and trusses of the night.
Our Daughters and Sons of the Saturated Fat
    (Who were nothing once and might have been again),
        Blame us as far afield as kissing cousins,
           Dead hussies and cads with unencumbered chattels.
Our Lady of Royal Jelly and Foot Cream
    (Who should have had salvation and may again),
        Take us spun-dry or awash, our bilges empty,
           And the salt-free ocean permanently pressed.
Our Father of the Slice and the Instant Transplant
    (Who had to be sworn in and suborned again),
        Forgive us our wakes and watches, turn us right
           Like dimmer-switches and thermostats at daybreak.
Our Ghost of the Clean Vacated Premises
    (Who was and is and never shall be again),
        Dispose us among the tone-deaf multitudes.
           Blink at our tears. Shine on our shrinking pupils.

3

THIS IS A WONDERFUL POEM

Come at it carefully, don't trust it, that isn't its right name,
It's wearing stolen rags, it's never been washed, its breath
Would look moss-green if it were really breathing,
It won't get out of the way, it stares at you
Out of eyes burnt gray as the sidewalk,
Its skin is overcast with colorless dirt,
It has no distinguishing marks, no I.D. cards,
It wants something of yours but hasn't decided
Whether to ask for it or just take it,
There are no policemen, no friendly neighbors,
No peacekeeping busybodies to yell for, only this
Thing standing between you and the place you were headed,
You have about thirty seconds to get past it, around it,
Or simply to back away and try to forget it,
It won't take no for an answer: try hitting it first
And you'll learn what's trembling in its torn pocket.
Now, what do you want to do about it?

CHORUS FROM A LOST PLAY — I

Again, we sing of man, the buckler of wind,
Tide-lifter, fire-stalker, ingenious crammer,
Inventor of death masks, nearsighted diver,
Proud maker of anthems to himself on sheepskin.

Where will his tongue not wag or his mind wander?
And what will he not take with his light fingers?
And who shall deny his birthright of safe plunder?
Has he not written in blood *I am the Master?*

Was he not born to meddle and mar forever?
Consider his majesty both standing and sitting:
His clever fingers hide from one another,
His bulging forehead broods on the world's egg.

Count his hard bargains, this plum-pruning grafter,
This flower-forcing gnome, sweet poisoner,
This keeper of blades, red-fingered sharpener.
What overlord can snatch away his laurel?

See him again careering through the country,
Outnumbered by the senses of other kingdoms:
The wary animals, sly vegetables,
And thick-veined minerals unearthed, unearthly.

Now see him stand at last in the barren valley
Surrounded by heaps of whalebone and plucked feathers,
By husks and roots from the dry pits of heaven.
Believer, worshipper, come close to touch him.

In the name of God, he'll dry your tears and kill you.

CHORUS FROM A LOST PLAY — II

Pity the masterless man. He lies by the road
Under our shade trees, neither coming nor going.
He folds his arms. He sits down by our river
Watching wild birds alight in the evening.

He sleeps and eats as he may and stoops to nothing.
He speaks before he is spoken to. He stares
When he should bow. He will not come when he's called.
Though arrows point the way, he will not follow.

Haven't we offered him our choicest masters
Who wear brave hats, who stamp themselves on silver,
Who preside in rooms with guards at every window
Commanding views that overlook our city?

How lonely to have no orders! How terrible
To bed down under a moon swelling and shrinking!
He keeps no schedules, suffers no opinions.
He has given up, yet he will not surrender.

Our clappers and gongs and sirens call to him;
He will not answer. Clockless and careless dreamer,
He pledges allegiance to unsanctioned demons
Housed in himself and disregards our fathers.

What can he do or be? Pity him. Damn him.

REPORT FROM A FOREST LOGGED BY THE WEYERHAEUSER COMPANY

Three square miles clear-cut.
Now only the facts matter:
The heaps of gray-splintered rubble,
The churned-up duff, the roots, the bulldozed slash,
The silence,

And beyond the ninth hummock
(All of them pitched sideways like wrecked houses)
A creek still running somewhere, bridged and dammed
By cracked branches.
No birdsong. Not one note.

And this is April, a sunlit morning.
Nothing but facts. Wedges like halfmoons
Fallen where saws cut over and under them
Bear ninety or more rings.
A trillium gapes at so much light.

Among the living: a bent huckleberry,
A patch of salal, a wasp,
And now, making a mistake about me,
Two brown-and-black butterflies landing
For a moment on my boot.

Among the dead: thousands of fir seedlings
A foot high, planted ten feet apart,
Parched brown for lack of the usual free rain,
Two buckshot beercans, and overhead,
A vulture big as an eagle.

Selective logging, they say, we'll take three miles,
It's good for the bears and deer, they say,
More brush and berries sooner or later,
We're thinking about the future—if you're in it
With us, they say. It's a comfort to say

Like *Dividend* or *Forest Management* or *Keep Out.*
They've managed this to a fare-thee-well.

In Chicago, hogs think about hog futures.
But staying with the facts, the facts,
I mourn with my back against a stump.

THE LESSON

That promising morning
Driving beside the river,
I saw twin newborn lambs
Still in a daze
At the grassy sunlight;
Beyond them, a day-old colt
As light-hoofed as the mare
That swayed over his muzzle—
Three staggering new lives
Above the fingerlings
From a thousand salmon nests—
And I sang on the logging road
Uphill for miles, then came
To a fresh two thousand acres
Of a familiar forest
Clear-cut and left for dead
By sawtoothed Weyerhaeuser.

I haunted those gray ruins
For hours, listening to nothing,
Being haunted in return
By vacancy, vacancy,
Till I grew as gray as stumps
Cut down to size. They drove me
Uphill, steeper and steeper,
Thinking: the salmon will die
In gillnets and crude oil,
The colt be broken and broken,
And the lambs leap to their slaughter.

I found myself in a rage
Two-thirds up Haystack Mountain
Being buzzed and ricochetted
By a metallic whir
That jerked me back toward life
Among young firs and cedars—
By a rufous hummingbird
Exulting in wild dives
For a mate perched out of sight

And cackling over and over,
Making me crouch and cringe
In his fiery honor.

ELEGY FOR A FOREST CLEAR-CUT BY THE WEYERHAEUSER COMPANY

Five months after your death, I come like the others
Among the slash and stumps, across the cratered
Three square miles of your graveyard:
Nettles and groundsel first out of the jumble,
Then fireweed and bracken
Have come to light where you, for ninety years,
Had kept your shadows.

The creek has gone as thin as my wrist, nearly dead
To the world at the dead end of summer,
Guttering to a pool where the tracks of an earth-mover
Showed it the way to falter underground.
Now pearly everlasting
Has grown to honor the deep dead cast of your roots
For a bitter season.

Those water- and earth-led roots decay for winter
Below my feet, below the fir seedlings
Planted in your place (one out of ten alive
In the summer drought) ,
Below the small green struggle of the weeds
For their own ends, below grasshoppers,
The only singers now.

The chains and cables and steel teeth have left
Nothing of what you were:
I hold my hands over a stump and remember
A hundred and fifty feet above me branches
No longer holding sway. In the pitched battle
You fell and fell again and went on falling
And falling and always falling.

Out in the open where nothing was left standing
 (The immoral equivalent of a forest fire),
I sit with my anger. The creek will move again,
Come rain and snow, gnawing at raw defiles,
Clear-cutting its own gullies.
As selective as reapers stalking through wheatfields,
Selective loggers go where the roots go.

SLEEPING IN THE WOODS

Not having found your way out of the woods, begin
Looking for somewhere to bed down at nightfall
Though you have nothing
But part of yourself to lie on, nothing but skin and backbone
And the bare ungiving ground to reconcile.
From standing to kneeling,
From crouching to turning over old leaves, to going under,
You must help yourself like any animal
To enter the charmed circle
Of the night with a body not meant for stretching or sprawling:
One ear-flap at a time knuckling your skull,
Your stiff neck (needing
An owl's twist to stay even) cross-purposing your spine,
With rigid ankles, with nowhere to put your arms.
But now, lying still
At last, you may watch the shadows seeking their own level,
The ground beneath you neither rising nor falling,
Neither giving nor taking
From the dissolving cadence of your heart, identical darkness
Behind and before your eyes—and you are going
To sleep without a ceiling,
For the first time without walls, not *falling* asleep, not losing
Anything under you to the imponderable
Dead and living
Earth, your countervailing bed, but settling down
Beside it across the slackening threshold
Of the place where it is always
Light, at the beginning of dreams, where the stars, shut out
By leaves and branches in another forest, burn
At the mattering source
Forever, though a dream may have its snout half sunk in blood
And the mind's tooth gnaw all night at bone and tendon
Among the trembling snares:
Whoever stumbles across you in the dark may borrow
Your hidebound substance for the encouragement
Of mites or angels;
But whatever they can't keep is yours for the asking. Turn up
In time, at the first faint stretch of dawn, and you'll see
A world pale-green as hazel,
The chalk-green convolute lichen by your hand like sea fog,

The fallen tree beside you in half-light
Dreaming a greener sapling,
The dead twigs turning over, and your cupped hand lying open
Beyond you in the morning like a flower.
Making light of it,
You have forgotten why you came, have served your purpose,
    and simply
By being here have found the right way out.
Now, you may waken.

FOR A WINTER WREN

In the first rain after a dry summer,
Small as a leaf, the color of fallen leaves,
You sang at the foot of a fallen cedar
Like a dream of singing, more quiet,
More intricate than the mass of stems
And moss-light roots you lighted on
Where the earth still clung to the dead, a song
Gentle and distant, nearly disappearing
Under the hush of the rain,
The soft trills rising out of next to nothing
To claim this side of silence.

BONSAI

(transplanted January 1973)

Four times before, this fir
Has turned from dirt to heaven, telling
Darkness from sunlight, stone from the gnarled air,
Rain falling from rain
Already fallen.

Its trunk, as twisted
As a root, was once a root,
Now split into five, reaching a mad balance
Against the memory of its bonsai masters:
Bulldozers, earth-movers.

Once, it was growing up-
Side down from an overhang, a stripped roadbank
Among the stumps of slaughtered and toppled others,
Wrenching itself, groping its way
Out of disaster.

Its buds are ready to burst
This spring, outward and upward, taking
One more turn between sky and a clutch of earth.
A frost-numbed bee clings to one stem
For dear life.

THE LOST STREET

"Just imagine: tomorrow morning you get in your car to
go to work. You start to pull out of the driveway, but—no
street."

—*What Highways Mean to You*
Auto Dealers Traffic Safety Council

You sit for a moment, idling, remembering
Another street running away from you
Before you learned to walk
Across it, even beside it: strange as a river
Under the elmtrees, it blurred
Uphill as far as the hospital
Or downhill into the dark city.

But this one, no longer stretching toward work,
Had been different, indifferent,
As easy to forget as a hall carpet
Leading from sleep to worry, from love
To bewilderment, from the steep hillside
Up to the greenhouse and the reservoir
Or down to the dimmed-out, burning city.

Now the deepening grass and brambles
Remind you there was somewhere you were going
Around the house instead of looking through glass
At this barely believable morning: you must get out
Of the car and stand on the ground,
Then kneel on it like a penitent gardener,
Touching it with your hands, crawling again to know it.

RAGING

Suddenly the stone tools spilled from the racks in my forehead.
I raged in the room, wanting to fall and wrestle through the floor
To the dirt, beside myself, myselves raking the air
As shaggy as half-men in a guttering kitchen midden.

But the door creaked open. We stood still
In opposite corners, drawing enough blood
To fill the darkened corners of our eyes,
While that sweet, reasonable third self
Came in and joined us like our motherwit.

The hard air melted out
Of our mouths, flowed out the window,
And came back soft as evening.
We drank it without speaking.

VACANCY

"We can think away objects, but not the space which they occupy."

—Einstein

The chair and table both go quietly;
The rug picks up its dust and disappears;
The floor and wallboards make room for the ceiling
To shut down on that thinker, alone at last
Among the point-blank furniture of his brain.

Do Not Write In This Space.

TRYING TO PRAY

My voice from its poor box
Enters the rank and file
Of voices mumbling prayers
From pew to nave to chancel,
As rank as any, as grating,
But rising no further
Than the head I've bent for it.

It raises no Father
From the stained broken glass
Strewn on my mind's eye,
No Son on a crutch,
No Ghost in Day-Glo,
Not even the Horny One
Hoofing it red-faced.

Instead, I hear the thump
Of knees against stone, half-see
Out of the squeezed corners
Of my eyes those squeezed in corners
By the crosshatched light
Asking for hope or help
Or maybe enough rope.

My one-way litany
Lies burning in my palms:
Tied to itself, the Self
May mutter trust or grief
Down through its crooked cave
And swallow the echo,
But true spelunkers go
On hands as well as knees
Till, face against rock face
In the votive darkness,
They touch what will not answer.

PRAYER

From this one breath,
By as many heartbeats
As my clenched fingers,
Make one inch of song.

4

Seven Songs for an Old Voice

FIRE SONG

I watch the point of the twirling stick
Where you are sleeping, where you will come again.
Already your breath, pale as fog through a vine-maple,
Is rising through shreds of cedarbark toward me.
Open your dark-red eye, Fire-brother.
Here is my breath to warm you. You may have all my breath.
Show me your yellow tongue, and I will feed you
Alder and black locust in thick branches
To gnaw in half like Beaver. Now, with you beside me,
I can see the eyes of the First People staring toward us
Hungrily, with the hollow look of Soul-catchers.
Hold them out at the thin edge of darkness, and I will keep you
As long and as well as I keep myself through the night.
Toward dawn, you may lie down slowly, drift slowly out of the
    ashes
To sleep again at the cold point of my spirit.

SONG FOR THE MAKER OF NIGHTMARES

You start your campfire on my breast like a mad grandfather
And eat my sleep for your food. Whenever you waken,
I must redden for war with your grunting children's children—
Thorn Cheek, Skinless Foot, Old Knife at the Lips, Moss Face,
Mouth-changer No One Hears, Lost Hand, my terrible brothers.
If you fall asleep in the middle of my fear, I come back
To claim my throat and my numb belly, like a dog
Who has strayed too far at night and swallowed his voice
At the first yawning of Bear Mother. Tonight I have no charms
To make you sleep. Begin again. Call out of their burrows
                      like woodworms
Stump, Mouse Woman, Snag, Split Man. Even in my terror
I must believe you: I will drink what you bring me in my broken
    skull,
The bitter water which once was sweet as morning.

SONG FOR THE SOUL GOING AWAY

I have wakened and found you gone
On a day torn loose from its moon, uprooted
And wilting. How can I call you back with dust in my mouth?
My words lie dead on the ground like leaves. Night speech,
Water speech, the speech of rushes and brambles
Have thinned to muttering and a vague crackle,
And the bird in my ribcage has turned black and silent.
Where a man would stand, I sit; where a man would sit,
I lie down burning; where a man would speak,
My voice shrinks backward into its dark hovel.
The dragonfly has taken his glitter from the pool,
Birds' eggs are stones, all berries wither.
Without you, my eyes make nothing of light and shadow,
And the cup of each eyelid has run dry.
I go as aimless as my feet among sticks and stones,
Thinking of you on your mad, bodiless journey.

DARK SONG

The faint scraping of stalk against leaf, the twig
And the caught thorn not quite breaking, yielding
Slowly in the night, are nothing
To fear: nothing knows
I am in this darkness, nothing knows which way
My dangerous eyes are turned. When young,
I bit the dark and clawed it, held my knife under its deep belly,
Set fire to it, jabbed it with sticks, strutted unseeing
Through its heart to my own rescue.
Now what stands behind my back is afraid:
I wait for longer than it can wait,
Listening, moving less than shadows.
It is mine now, soft as the breath of owls.

SONG FOR THE SOUL RETURNING

Without singing, without the binding of midnight,
Without leaping or rattling, you have come back
To lodge yourself in the deep fibres under my heart,
More closely woven than a salmonberry thicket.
I had struck the rocks in your name, but no one answered;
Left empty under the broken wings of the sun,
I had tasted and learned nothing. Now the creek no longer
Falters from stone to stone with a dead fishtailing
But bursts like the ledges of dawn, the east and west winds
Meet on the hillside, and the softening earth
Spreads wide for my feet where they have never dared to go.
Out of the silent holts of willow and hazel, the wild horses,
Ears forward, come toward us, hearing your voice rise
    from my mouth.
My hands, whose craft had disappeared, search out each other
To shelter the warm world returning between them.

SONG FOR THE FIRST PEOPLE

When you learned that men were coming, you changed into rocks,
Into fish and birds, into flowers and rivers in despair of us.
The tree under which I bend may be you,
That stone by the fire, the nighthawk swooping
And crying out over the swamp reeds, the reeds themselves.
Have I held you too lightly all my mornings?
I have broken your silence, dipped you up
Carelessly in my hands and drunk you, burnt you,
Carved you, slit your calm throat and danced on your skin,
Made charms of your bones. You have endured
All of it, suffering my foolishness
As the old wait quietly among clumsy children.
Now others are coming, neither like you nor like men.
I must change, First People. How do I change myself?
If no one can teach me the long will of the cedar,
Let me become Water Dog, Bitterroot, or Shut Beak.
Change me. Forgive me. I will learn to crawl, stand, or fly
Anywhere among you, forever, as though among great elders.

DEATH SONG

I touch the earth on all fours like a child,
And now my forehead touches the earth.
For the sake of my joys, Sleepmaker, let me in.
I have turned away from none of the six directions.
I have praised the rising and the dying wind,
Water falling or vanishing, even the end of grass.
I have welcomed the seasons equally
And been one with all weather from the wild to the silent.
The only blood left on my hands is my own: now my heart
Will be strict, admitting none, letting none go.
Close all my mouths. I will sleep inside of sleep,
Honoring the gift of darkness till it breaks.
I sing for a cold beginning.

NEW POEMS
(1976)

BREAKING CAMP

Having spent a hard-earned sleep, you must break camp in the
      mountains
At the break of day, pulling up stakes and packing,
Scattering your ashes,
And burying everything human you can't carry. Lifting
Your world now on your shoulders, you should turn
To look back once
At a place as welcoming to a later dead-tired stranger
As it was to your eyes only the other evening,
As the place you've never seen
But must hope for now at the end of a day's rough journey:
You must head for another campsite, maybe no nearer
Wherever you're going
Than where you've already been, but deeply, starkly appealing
Like a lost home: with water, the wind lying down
On a stretch of level earth,   ˙
And the makings of a fire to flicker against the night
Which you, travelling light, can't bring along
But must always search for.

MEETING A BEAR

If you haven't made noise enough to warn him, singing, shouting,
Or thumping sticks against trees as you walk in the woods,
Giving him time to vanish
  (As he wants to) quietly sideways through the nearest thicket,
You may wind up standing face to face with a bear.
Your near future,
Even your distant future, may depend on how he feels
Looking at you, on what he makes of you
And your upright posture
Which, in his world, like a down-swayed head and humped
     shoulders,
Is a standing offer to fight for territory
And a mate to go with it.
Gaping and staring directly are as risky as running:
To try for dominance or moral authority
Is an empty gesture,
And taking to your heels is an invitation to a dance
Which, from your point of view, will be no circus.
He won't enjoy your smell
Or anything else about you, including your ancestors
Or the shape of your snout. If the feeling's mutual,
It's still out of balance:
He doesn't *care* what you think or calculate; your disapproval
Leaves him as cold as the opinions of salmon.
He may feel free
To act out all his own displeasures with a vengeance:
You would do well to try your meekest behavior,
Standing still
As long as you're not mauled or hugged, your eyes downcast.
But if you must make a stir, do everything sidelong,
Gently and naturally,
Vaguely oblique. Withdraw without turning and start saying
Softly, monotonously, whatever comes to mind
Without special pleading:
Nothing hurt or reproachful to appeal to his better feelings.
He has none, only a harder life than yours.
There's no use singing
National anthems or battle hymns or alma maters
Or any other charming or beastly music.
Use only the dullest,

Blandest, most colorless, undemonstrative speech you can think of,
Bears, for good reason, find it embarrassing
Or at least disarming
And will forget their claws and cover their eyeteeth as an answer.
Meanwhile, move off, yielding the forest floor
As carefully as your honor.

WALKING IN A SWAMP

When you first feel the ground under your feet
Going soft and uncertain,
It's best to start running as fast as you can slog
Even though falling
Forward on your knees and lunging like a cripple.
You may escape completely
Being bogged down in those few scampering seconds.
But if you're caught standing
In deep mud, unable to walk or stagger,
It's time to reconsider
Your favorite postures, textures, and means of moving,
Coming to even terms
With the kind of dirt that won't take no for an answer.
You must lie down now,
Like it or not: if you're in it up to your thighs,
Be seated gently,
Lie back, open your arms, and dream of floating
In a sweet backwater.
Slowly your sunken feet will rise together,
And you may slither
Spread-ottered casually backwards out of trouble.
If you stay vertical
And, worse, imagine you're in a fearful struggle,
Trying to swivel
One stuck leg at a time, keeping your body
Above it all,
Immaculate, you'll sink in even deeper,
Becoming an object lesson
For those who wallow after you through the mire,
In which case you should know
For near-future reference: muck is one part water,
One part what-have-you,
Including yourself, now in it over your head,
As upright as ever.

TRACKING

The man ahead wasn't expecting you
To follow: he was careless
At first, dislodging stones, not burying ashes,
Forgetting his heelmarks,
Lighting his fires by night to be seen for miles,
Breaking dead silence.
But he's grown wary now: in this empty country
You must learn to read
What you've never read before: the minute language
Of moss and lichen,
The signals of bent grass, the speech of sand,
The gestures of dust.
No man can move two feet from where he is,
Lightfooted or lame,
Without disturbing the natural disorder
Under him always,
And no sly sweeping with branches, no bootless dodging,
No shifting to hardpan,
Not even long excursions across bedrock
Should trick your attention.
If you come to running water, head upstream:
Everything human
Climbs as it runs away and goes to ground later.
What tries to escape you
Will count on you to suffer discouragement,
And so, at dogged last,
If you've shuffled off the deliberate evasions
And not been sidetracked,
Have followed even blind trails, cutting for sign
Through slides and washouts,
You should be prepared for that unwelcome meeting:
The other, staring
Back to see who's made this much of his footprints,
To study your dead-set face
And find out whether you mean to kill him, join him,
Or simply to blunder past.

MISSING THE TRAIL

Only a moment ago you were thinking of something
Different, the sky or yesterday or the wind,
But suddenly it's yourself
Alone, strictly alone, having taken a wrong turn
Somewhere behind you, having missed the trail,
Bewildered, now uncertain
Whether to turn back, bear left or right, or flounder ahead
Stubbornly, breaking new ground out of pride or panic,
Or to raise your voice
Out of fear that screaming is the only universal language.
If you come to your senses, all six, taking your time,
The spot where you're standing
Is your best hope. When it first dawns on you you're lost,
You must memorize everything around you, scouring
That place for landmarks,
For rocks, bushes, or trees you'd know again in the dark,
For anything unmistakable to return to,
Or some ragged signal
That can reestablish your eyes, even the shirt off your back,
While you branch out from there, the trunk of your life,
In all directions,
Trying to stumble once more across the vaguest of trails
You may want to follow again for some strange reason
Toward somewhere or other
You may now (having been lost and found) barely remember
Wanting to get to, past the middle of nowhere,
Toward your wit's end.

FROM HERE TO THERE

Though you can see in the distance, outlined precisely
With speechless clarity, the place you must go,
The problem remains
Judging how far away you are and getting there safely.
Distant objects often seem close at hand
When looked at grimly,
But between you and those broken hills (so sharply in focus
You have to believe in them with all your senses)
Lies a host of mirages:
Water put out like fire, the shimmer of flying islands,
The unbalancing act of mountains upside down.
Passing through too much air,
Light shifts, fidgets, and veers in ways clearly beyond you,
Confusing its weights and measures with your own
Which are far simpler:
A man on foot can suffer only one guiding principle
Next to his shadow: One Damn Thing After Another,
Meaning his substance
In the shape of his footsoles against the unyielding ground.
When you take a step, whatever you ask to bear you
Is bearing your life:
Sound earth may rest on hollow earth, and stones too solid
To budge in one direction may be ready
To gather no moss
With you, end over end, in another. You've been foolhardy
Enough already to make this slewfooted journey
Through a place without pathways
Where looking back seems as disheartening as relearning
The whole mad lay of the land by heart
After an earthquake.
At last, watching your step, having shrugged off most illusions,
And stumbling close enough to rap your knuckles
Against the reality
Of those unlikely rocks you've stared at through thick
 and thin
Air and the dumb-shows of light, your hope should be,
As a hardened traveller,
Not to see your trembling hands passing through cloud-stuff,
Some flimsy mock-up of a world spun out of vapor,

But to find yourself
In the Land Behind the Wind where nothing is the matter
But you, brought to your knees, an infirm believer
Asking one more lesson.

BEING SHOT

You'll hear it split-seconds later—the loud afterthought
Booming among tree trunks like a thunder-crack
To startle ravens
And suddenly lift moose-racks dripping with waterlilies
For miles around—unless you're too involved,
Too strangely preoccupied
With absorbing the impact of this bullet, in sharp contrast
With your soft flesh and blood, your yielding sinew,
Your tractable bones.
If it hasn't broken your heart or skull, this bit of metal
May strike you as a blunder, a senseless burden,
An appalling intrusion
Into your privacy, to which your body, turning, may take
Vigorous exception, but soon you'll feel it growing
Heavy, then heavier,
And if you haven't fallen involuntarily, you may
Volunteer now and find what ease waits here
On the forest floor,
The duff of sword fern and sorrel, of spike moss and beadruby
That takes without question whatever comes its way,
While you begin to study
At first hand now the symptoms of shock: the erratic heartbeat,
The unexpected displeasure of half-breathing,
The coming of the cold,
The tendency to forget exactly why you're sprawling somewhere
That has slipped your mind for a moment, seeing things
In a new light
Which doesn't come from the sky but from all loose ends
Of all your hopes, your dissolving endeavors
To keep close track
Of who you are, and where you had started from, and why
You were walking in the woods before this stranger
(Who is leaning over you
Now with a disarming smile) interfered so harshly.
Not wishing to make yourself conspicuous
By your endless absence
And having meant no harm by moving quietly, searching
Among this second growth of your own nature
For its first wildness,
You may offer him your empty hands, now red as his hat,

And he may grant mercy or, on the other hand,
Give you as gracefully
As time permits, as lack of witnesses will allow
Or your punctured integrity will stand for,
A graceful *coup de grace*.

WAITING IN A RAIN FOREST

The rain does not fall here: it stands in the air around you
Always, drifting from time to time like breath
And gathering on the leaf-like
Pale shield lichen as clearly as the intricate channels
Along the bloc .wort gleaming like moths' eyes,
Out of the maidenhair
And the running pine and the soft small towers of club moss
Where you must rest now under a green sky
In a land without flowers
Where the wind has fixed its roots and the motionless weather
Leaves you with nothing to do but watch the unbroken
Promises of the earth
And know whatever lies down, like you or a fallen nurse-log,
Will taste the deepest longing of young hemlocks
And learn without fear or favor
This gentlest of undertakings: moss mending your ways
While many spring from one to a wild garden
Flourishing in silence.

TRAVELLING LIGHT

Through this most difficult country, this world we had known
As a cross-grained hummocky bog-strewn jumble of brambles
Stretching through summer,
We find after blizzard and sunlight, travelling in the winter,
A rolling parkland under our snowshoes
Where every color
Has drifted out of our shadows into a brittle whiteness.
And so we begin shuffling our way forward
Above the invisible
Deadfalls and pitfallen brush, above the deeply buried
Landmarks and blazes we had found misleading,
Above the distraction
Of flowers and sweet berries and bird-songs that held us
Back, breathing and tasting, sitting, listening.
Now we are hurrying
With the smooth swift scuttling of webs, our feet not touching
The earth, our breath congealing, our ears hearing
More than we can believe in
In the denser air: disembodied by the cold, the shouting,
Shouting from miles away, the slamming of gunfire,
The ghosts of axes.
But, by tonight, we must learn the serious art of sleeping,
Of lying down, not going on nerve alone
To court exhaustion
Which, here in the deep snow, is another name for forever.
We will make fire, then turn in each other's arms,
Embracing once more
All we have brought this far in our raw-hided fiber,
By rock, by river, by ourselves under the branches
Of this living firtree
Where, unlike us, the grouse may perch through a whole winter.
And then the cold-spelled morning will make us stare
Into each other's eyes
For the first signs of whiteness, stare at the ends of fingers,
Then into the distance where the whitening
Marks the beginning
Of the place we were always looking for: so full of light,
So full of flying light, it is all feathers
Which we must wear
As we had dreamed we would, not putting frostbitten hands

Into the freshly slaughtered breasts of birds
But snowblindly reaching
Into this dazzling white-out, finding where we began,
Not naming the wonder yet but remembering
The simply amazing
World of our first selves where believing is once more seeing
The cold speech of the earth in the colder air
And knowing it by heart.

2

THE FIRST TRICK

Onstage, the Professor in a brilliant spotlight
Takes our applause. Nothing has happened yet.
In a moment he'll produce something from nothing,
Make something vanish, seem to commit mayhem
On the lovely lady standing beyond him,
And prove us wrong or gravely misdirected,
While he, in league with rabbits and white doves,
With flags stuffed up his sleeves, has all the answers.
We sit in rows, our chairs screwed to the floor,
Our tickets torn in half, staring through darkness.

THE RETURN OF ICARUS

He showed up decades later, crook-necked and hip-sprung,
Not looking for work but cadging food and wine as artfully
As a king, while our dogs barked themselves inside out
At the sight of his hump and a whiff of his goatskin.

We told him Daedalus was dead, worn out with honors
(Some of them fabulous) , but especially for making
Wings for the two of them and getting them off the ground.
He said he remembered that time, but being too young a
        mooncalf,

He hadn't cared about those labyrinthine double-dealings
Except for the scary parts, the snorting and bellowing.
He'd simply let the wax be smeared over his arms
And suffered handfuls of half-stuck second-hand chicken feathers

And flapped and flapped, getting the heft of them, and taken
Off (to both their amazements), listening for his father's
Endless, garbled, and finally inaudible instructions
From further and further below, and then swooping

And banking and trying to hover without a tail and stalling
While the old man, a slow learner, got the hang of it.
At last, with the weight of his years and his genius,
Daedalus thrashed aloft and was gawkily airborne.

And they went zigzagging crosswind and downwind over the
        water,
Half-baked by the sirocco, with Daedalus explaining
Everything now: which way was up, how to keep your mouth
Shut for the purpose of breathing and listening,

How to fly low (having no choice himself) in case of Harpies,
And how to keep Helios beaming at a comfortable distance
By going no higher than the absolute dangling minimum
To avoid kicking Poseidon, the old salt, square in the froth.

But Icarus saw the wax at his skinny quill-tips sagging,
And he couldn't get a word in edgewise or otherwise,

So he strained even higher, searching for ships or landfalls
While he still had time to enjoy his share of the view,

And in the bright, high-spirited silence, he took comfort
From his father's lack of advice, and Helios turned
Cool, not hot as Icarus rose, joining a wedge of geese
For an embarrassing, exhilarating moment northward,

And then grew cold till the wax turned brittle as marble,
Stiffening his elbows and suddenly breaking
Away, leaving him wingless, clawing at nothing, then falling
Headfirst with a panoramic, panchromatic vista

Of the indifferent sun, the indifferent ocean, and a blurred
Father passing sideways, still chugging and flailing away
With rows of eagle feathers. When Icarus hit the water,
He took its salt as deeply as his own.

He didn't tell us how he'd paddled ashore or where
He'd been keeping himself or what in the world he'd been doing
For a living, yet he didn't seem bitter. "Too bad
You weren't around," we said, "there'd have been something in it

For you, probably—an apartment straddling an aqueduct,
Orchards, invitations, hecatombs of women."
"No hard feelings," he said. "Wings weren't *my* idea."
And he told odd crooked stories to children for hours

About what lived under water, what lived under the earth,
And what still lived in the air, and why. A few days later
He slouched off on his game leg and didn't come back.
He didn't steal any chickens or girls' hearts

Or ask after his father's grave or his father's money
Or even kick the dogs. But he showed us calluses
Thicker than hooves on his soles and palms, and told us
That's how he'd stay in touch, keeping his feet on the ground.

ROLES

Old enough then to know
Better, I still wondered:
Could I be a spy, an actor,
Or a hard ship's captain?
What startling hats and shoes
Would I dare squeeze into?

Performance after performance
In public or deadly private
I dreamed my self-contained
Self in the dead center
Of dangerous attention:
Swift exit and entrance
In romance after romance—
Sinking in the tradition
Or being half-shot at dawn
Or timing my best breath
Through a final curtain.

Gentlemen, you've retired.
You're welcome to tend your gardens
In the back of my mind.
Like you, I've worked odd hours
And felt, in the odder years,
Disowned by superiors;
Like you, went far from home.
Over our back fence
Give me your worst advice
And your harshest judgments.
I've become a man in a room
Marking time on paper.

GETTING SOMEWHERE

All summer, that water shimmering
Would call me to the ends of streets
Where there was no water,
The flat heat-shimmer fading
And going patchy if I went near: no river
To cross, no way to drink there.

I would see my father
And all the others fording quicksilver,
Wavering home in pieces, in swollen cars
Or collapsing on stilts, their profiles wobbly
But turning harder as they came closer
Out of a spilled mirror.

Bent upward over my head that summer,
Light had somewhere better to go
For its hard labor, leaving mock water
Between me and all distance, keeping
Its distance, running or standing,
As out of reach as a rainbow.

THE DEATH OF PAUL BUNYAN

No common death, not some civilized garden variety,
After he'd raised sweet hell from the minute he was born:
Growing two feet a day on the milk of fourteen cows,
Uprooting one-handed a full-grown pinetree and, half-grown,
Swinging his unbelievable ax in the woods till the blade melted.

He didn't need a plot in some marble orchard, memorizing
The out-of-business-ends of daisies forever. Hadn't he taken
Babe the Blue Ox, his meaty darling, who was forty-two
　　ax-handles
And a plug of tobacco between the horns, and chained her
To the bend of a crooked road and yanked it straight?

With a voice that could dam rivers and mortify thunder
Hadn't he called together the wildest, most lumbering lumber
　　camp
Ever dreamed of?—timber beasts in their stagged overalls
Whose boots could go galloping straight up the trunks of firs,
Men nine feet to the lowest limb and five feet through at the butt?

In the Winter of Blue Snow, when the temperature sank
Forty feet below zero, when music and men's words froze
And lay around in clumps and blue streaks, good for nothing,
Hadn't he hitched Babe to the Temperate Zone and goaded
And bullwhacked her far enough north for a thawing out?

And hadn't he dug the St. Lawrence, the Grand Canyon,
　　Puget Sound?
And chopped down in a week all the trees in North Dakota?
And hadn't his huge empty laughter gone bellowing
Down every skidroad between the Cascades and the Olympics
Till it seemed as natural as a load of logs hitting a log dump?

So, having done everything any boss could ask for, he quit,
Laid himself off, took Babe high into the virgin forest
To fish and hunt and laze around and maybe even think
Once in a while when he could think of something to think of
And sleep and eat, a retired giant whittling a few cedars.

But they came after him, a new breed of skyline loggers
(Who didn't even know he was there), the donkey punchers

With their engines and whistle punks, the rigging slingers
Lashing their high-lead tackle taller than any legend
With whining of cables, clanking of chains, yowling of chainsaws:

Not single jacks alone in the unending woods
But smaller men who had never stunk out a bunkhouse
Or roared themselves hoarse while gandy-dancing
Around the walls of Speckle-belly Kate's, who couldn't birl
A log while rotgut rolled through their own heartwood.

They caught him and Babe asleep and cut them down
    with the trees,
Not knowing the difference among the billions of board feet
And the mountains of slashed boughs where the bulldozed duff
And ferns went upside down in the rain, where stumps of any
    kind,
Trees or giants, looked alike and were a dime a million.

What happened to him after that was a dirty pity:
He hit the skids to a log pond, went to pieces, split
This way and that, rough cut, quartered, shingled,
Pulped, sawdusted, half-seasoned, down-graded, planked
And nailed up and down at the mercy of wood butchers.

But far out in the forest, his fellow creatures
That didn't know any better or any worse,
Being helpless now without someone to dream them,
Began lamenting: his tote-road shagamaw
Shaking its grizzly paws and moosey haunches;

The sausagy walapaloosie, mushy as mushrooms;
The snow snake, the rumptifusel, the gumberoo
That would burst near campfires, the fishy billdad,
The redoubtable splinter cat, and the mourning squonk
Wept loud and long for Paul Bunyan, then faded forever.

THE BREAKING POINT

There are four kinds of stress,
Yet we are not concerned
Today with compression,
Torsion, or simple bending
But (for this unknown substance
No wider than your spine)
Strictly with tension:
You will notice the sample
Is clamped at either end
By a framework designed
To measure the exact strain
Required to break it: this
Experiment might be crucial
To you: if you can learn
Under careful control
At what stress it will fail,
You are forewarned and -armed
Against one small disaster;
Therefore, not knowing
The breaking point
Precisely we begin increasing
Tension, at first seeing
Nothing, but soon on the surface
A change, an ashen look
As the crystal structure goes
Amorphous, and suddenly
The irreversible thinning
Out, the elastic failure,
The crack, the full fracture
At a waist like an hourglass,
The gauge spinning to zero,
And the two jagged halves
Never to be made one
Again except through fire
And the founding hammer.

WALKING AT NIGHT

After the sidewalk, after the last streetlight at the end
Of concrete crumbling into thickening weeds, I begin
Shuffling slowly off balance, my shadow's feet gone slipshod
Under mine, as it stretches further and further into the night,
Now spindly, fading to nothing as quickly as I darken.

I move, my legs more lost than in a swamp, going blind
Among the dead calm branches of a bush that knows
Where its thorns belong, blundering star-nosed as a mole
Through rubble, slanting and slumping, shortcutting myself
For no good reason: the last light shines where I abandoned it.

No wings, no antennae, no burning catch-all eyes, no echoes
Whistling back from the shapes out of my reach, no starlight
Scratching a line of march over the smudged heavens:
Nothing but streaks of cloud being rushed blue-gray as steel
Across the slammed vault of the sky, a moonless coffer,

Where the only guides are the heart in my mouth, my body's
    guesswork,
And sticks crackling under my feet as if in a dark fire.

RELICS

. . . the terrible hunger for objects. . . .

—Roethke

Leaning against my books, the sunflowers
Wait with their heavy heads bent deeper now
Than when I uprooted them
Cold months ago, their corollas ragged
Around the arcs of seeds, their stalks hardened,
Their leaves as stiff as the broom-stiff roots
Dusting the floor that holds us above ground.

I grew them from the heads of their lost grandfathers
And keep them with me like the gleanings
Of a harvest, for the sake of what *they* keep,
Not weary of time, though ready to do without
The sun, their dazzling, disappearing master,
For as long as I keep this roof over our heads
And keep my own head at the onset of winter.

In my study, while days shorten and darken,
I count what else I've gathered around me:
The goat's jawbone, porcupine teeth, clutches of barnacles,
The nest of a fox sparrow, the slashed wing of a teal,
The stuffed young golden eagle older than I am,
The crosscut slab of cedar from a dead forest,
And these sunflowers, like the relics of ancestors.

Help me now, old goat-beard, slow spiny-back,
Chalk-mouthed sea-eaters, clear singer in thickets,
Marsh-skimmer, sky-toucher, heart of heartwood,
And you sun-gazers, now bent on a long night-watch,
Leaning against my books and pieces of books
And pieces of poems and disembodied words,
Your heads heavy with promises for another season.

FOR A THIRTEENTH ANNIVERSARY

Through that weddingless hour
When our sole witness,
A garage mechanic, was late,
And the Justice of the Peace
At the first sign of distress
Said, "Take her into the garden,"
I wilted with you and waited
By hornets and slug-bait
While you held the trembling nosegay
I'd barely remembered to buy
From a shop at a graveyard.

I strained for words and sweated
And knew (by the sagging cosmos
And sunburnt hollyhocks)
I'd always feel like a toad,
But hoped you wouldn't notice
The miserable distance
Between me and the Prince
Lost in your heart's dungeon,
Though I swore I'd find the way
Down through that cobbled passage
And rescue him and haul him
Up into daylight
Where you wouldn't have to choose
But could bear us both, the one
For agony and romance,
The other, comic relief,
Where we could live forever
In our own ramshackle garden
With aphids and leaf-rollers
Among the unpruned roses
And see our apple blossoms
Festooned by caterpillars.

HER DREAM

She breathes, lying flat in the night, catches her breath
And holds it, starting, stopping, suddenly turning
To the wall, to the ceiling for their coldest comfort,
Lets out all breath as if done with it,
Then after a dead moment, after the hours
Of wrestling with her pain, she begins deep, steady breathing.

I lie beside her, listening
And staring at the clenched hands of the clock, counting
A prayer to the God of Numbers to lead her
Down out of harm, to healing within healing
Without me, even without herself to follow
Into darkness softer than her pillow.

She breathes more deeply. I catch myself
Napping, then snap awake. The clock is in gauze. Her breath
Comes quick and shallow
With the sudden abrupt pauses of a dreamer,
The muffled laughter and whimpers from the other room
        of her sleep,
From the lurching corridor, the sinking stairwell,

And I turn to her and follow her
And blunder into her dream where the cackling women
Claw with their broken nails, where the hooded,
        berserk warlocks
Slash at us both in vain, where the mad dwarves can't betray us,
Where we float through the wreckage of our shadows,
Breathing till morning.

AT LOW TIDE

To the first inch of the sea, we come like shorebirds—
To water sliding away
From limpets holding fast among barnacles
As stone-like as the stones they were born to.

In the mud underfoot we search again
Among the feasting and dying for the salvage
Of the clam's half-shell or the whelk's redeeming mouth
Or the sheath of the moon snail melting to its beginning.

As we touch, we breathe or forget our breath,
See and go blind, but see
Our love once more in the salt brimming our eyelids
Where nothing is lost, where the tide turns over and over.

CLANCY

We bought him at auction, tranquillized to a drooping halt,
A blue-roan burro to be ridden by infants in arms, by tyros
Or the feeblest ladies, to be slapped or curried or manhandled,
A burro for time exposures, an amiable lawnmower.

But he burst out of his delivery truck like a war horse,
Figure-eighting all night at the end of his swivel chain,
Chin high, octuple-gaited, heehawing through two octaves
Across our field and orchard, over the road, over the river.

While I fenced-in our farm to keep him from barnstorming
Neighbors and dignified horses, then palisaded our house
Like a beleaguered fort, my wife with sugar and rolled oats
And mysteries of her own coaxed him slowly into her favor.

He stood through the muddiest weather, spurning all shelter,
Archenemy of gates and roofs, mangler of halters,
Detector of invisible hackamores, surefooted hoofer
Against the plots of strangers or dogs or the likes of me.

But she would brush him and whisper to him out of earshot
And feed him hazel branches and handfuls of blackberries
And run and prance beside him, while he goated and
        buck-jumped,
Then stood by the hour with his long soft chin on her shoulder

While I was left on the far side of my own fence
Under the apple trees, playing second pitchfork
Among a scattering of straw over the dark-gold burro-apples
Too powerful for any garden, even the Hesperides.

And I still watch from exile as, night or morning, they wander
Up slope and down without me, neither leading nor following
But simply taking their time over the important pasture,
Considering dew and cobwebs and alfalfa and each other.

And all his ancestors, once booted through mountain passes
Bearing their grubstaked packtrees, or flogged up dusty arroyos
To their bitter ends without water, are grazing now in the bottom
Of her mind and his, digesting this wild good fortune.

FOR PATT, WHISPERING TO A BURRO

One arm around his neck, she whispers
Into his unpromising, uncompromising ear
What I may never discover:
In the middle of a field, she tells him
What they have always remembered,
Something as nameless as the calmest day
Ever to drift through fences,
Something they lost once
In the swelter of hard mountains,
In the blizzards drifting
Over the gold-burdened rivers,
Something they may never find
Again but will always search for:
Not magic words spell-breaking or -binding
But the first spell itself, the enduring
Dream between her lips and his ear,
As round-eyed, as constant,
As sure as they stand together.

THE OLD WORDS

This is hard to say
Simply, because the words
Have grown so old together:
Lips and *eyes* and *tears,*
Touch and *fingers*
And *love,* out of love's language,
Are hard and smooth as stones
Laid bare in a streambed,
Not failing or fading
Like the halting speech of the body
Which will turn too suddenly
To ominous silence,
But like your lips and mine
Slow to separate, our fingers
Reluctant to come apart,
Our eyes and their slow tears
Reviving like these words
Springing to life again
And again, taken to heart,
To touch, love, to begin.

THE UNCANNY ILLUSION OF THE
HEADLESS LADY

The curtains part. We see a headless lady
Sitting alone, one hand on a tabletop,
The other resting palm-up in her lap.
Red tubes are pouring bubbles into her neck.
As ladylike as can be, shifting her thighs,
She waves at us with the lonely tips of her fingers.

Beyond the footlights, must we settle for less
Than everything about her, losing her voice
And the hair we've never known and her parted lips?
Though she can't see us, won't she find us touching
Here as we strain for one clear glance at her face
Among the glancing blows of her limelight?

But now the curtains close. If we rush backstage,
Will we find her, after all, eating a sandwich
With a real mouth, her nose in a magazine?
Or does she stay forever at that table,
Imbibing through tubes some heavenly elixir
In a world we couldn't dream of without mirrors?

3

THE CHANGE

Sometimes, when no one watches, Grizzly Bear turns into
a man.
                                   —Northwest Indian belief

He glares at the white hand in front of his face
Where teeth fall short of lips, where a thick tongue
Falls even shorter of a nose telling him nothing,
Nothing upwind but numbness.

His eyes see far too much, too far
Over the valley where only his claws mattered,
But something huge has gone to sleep in him
As deep as winter.

His stomach turns to a cave in this raw morning,
Empty and gaping: the sound coming out of his mouth
Is thin as blood, as thin as dying,
The last bleat of a lamb.

And in the strange high fearful head the spasms
Reach through the naked neck, through the naked spine,
Through the naked haunches, setting his hindlegs stumbling,
Stumbling and running.

WHO SHALL BE THE SUN?

The People said, "Who shall be the sun?"
Raven cried, "Raven! Raven!"
He imagined rising and setting
Grandly, his great wings spreading over the People.
All days would belong to him. No one
Would see the earth without marvelous Raven.

He rose then out of the thick night.
He crooked his ragged wings, flapping them wildly,
Yet he made evening all day long,
Nothing but gloom in the woods, shade on the rivers.
The People grunted: "Get away from the sky!
You are too dark! Come down, foolish Raven!"

The People said, "Someone else must try."
Hawk screamed, "Hawk! Hawk!"
He imagined rising and rising
High over the specks of the tiny People.
He would be alone, taller than the wind. No one
Would cast a shadow without brilliant Hawk.

He rose then out of the empty night.
He soared and climbed into the yellow air
As high as noon, clenching his talons,
His bright wings flashing in the eye of the heavens.
The People squinted and shouted: "Too much daylight!
Get out of the sky! Come down, ignorant Hawk!"

The People said, "But we must have someone."
Coyote howled, "Coyote! Coyote!"
He imagined jumping and running
Low over the bent heads of the People.
He would make them crouch all day. No one
Would escape the tricks of clever Coyote.

He rose then out of the hole of night.
He darted and leaped over the red clouds
As swift as stormfire, his jaws gleaming,
His wild breath burning over the crowns of trees.
The People sweated and sputtered, diving into water,
"You will cook the earth! Come down, crazy Coyote!"

The People said, "We shall have no sun at all!"
But Snake whispered, "I have dreamed I was the sun."
Raven, Hawk, and Coyote mocked him by torchlight:
"You cannot scream or howl! You cannot run or fly!
You cannot burn, dazzle, or blacken the earth!
How can you be the sun?" "By dreaming," Snake whispered.

He rose then out of the rich night.
He coiled in a ball, low in the sky.
Slowly he shed the Red Skin of Dawn,
The Skin of the Blue Noontime, the Skin of Gold,
And last the Skin of Darkness, and the People
Slept in their lodges, safe, till he coiled again.

HOW MOSS GREW STRONG

Ice shouted, "My sons must be the strongest of sons!
They must knock down all the trees standing against me!"
Each day, with North Wind, he drove them into the ocean
To harden their bodies, shaking with fever.
Each day he watched them wrestle with saplings,
Panting and grunting, wrenching but not breaking.

"Stronger!" Ice shouted. He doused them with freezing water
And made them run with rocks lashed to their feet
Till his sons were weak and angry—all but Moss.
Moss grew in a corner of his father's house
And would not stand in the ocean or trudge with stones.
His brothers were jealous. They said, "Moss is afraid."

Moss said, "I have no enemies." Ice shouted,
"If you have no enemies, you have no father!"
And he scattered Moss into the deepest woods
Where he lay down at the feet of the great trees
On the side of North Wind, in rain and snow,
And, with strong arms, wrestled with them forever.

HOW STONE HELD HIS BREATH

Ice shouted, "My sons are stealing my breath!"
From among them, he picked Stone
And squeezed him white as the moon,
Ground him on cliffsides, dragged him down canyons.

"See what becomes of thieves!" Ice shouted
And pitched him through crackling rivers,
Dropped him into the hard nest of his mouth
And gnawed him with hailstones.

Ice herded his other sons up mountains.
Under four winds, under the spilled rain,
Under the red foxtail of the sun,
Stone lay still, holding his cold breath.

HOW STUMP STOOD IN THE WATER

Ice had many sons. "Find me my food!" he shouted.
They searched in the air and under the water
And brought him Quail and Mussel, Goose and Oyster,
Blue Teal and Rock Crab, Widgeon and Salmon.

"More! More!" Ice shouted. "My sons must feed me!"
Some climbed after Eagle and fell. Some paddled
After Gray Whale and drowned. Some offered
Buzzard and Minnow, Coot and Sea Slug.

But Stump stood in the ocean, catching nothing.
"Foolish Stump!" Ice shouted. "What are you standing on?
What are you holding in your shut hands?
Feed me! Feed me!" But Stump said, "Father,

What am I standing on? What am I holding?
If you tell me, they will be yours forever."
Ice shouted, "You are standing on Flounder!
You have stolen the last sweet eggs of Killdeer

For your selfish dinner! The tide is rising!
Who brings me nothing will come to nothing!"
Then Ice pulled back his other sons to the north,
And the water rose, and the water ebbed away,

And on the barren shore, Stump stood alone
On his own feet, holding his life in his hands.

HOW STUMP FOUND HIS VILLAGE

Stump went from lodge to river, the loud one,
From woods to swamp, the stone-thrower, stick-jabber,
Thief of all eyes and ears, wanting to stand
Where anyone else was standing, wanting no one
To hide from him, no one to be alone.

If someone breathed, Stump wanted that same air.
If someone drank, Stump wanted that water.
If someone dreamed, Stump wanted that whole dream in his belly.
He wanted the sharp teeth of Weasel, Magpie's feathers,
Wanted to wear the long quick skin of Blue Racer.

Weasel said, "Reeds, Reeds, whisper to Stump."
Magpie said, "Reeds, call Stump away
Through the green sunlight falling under your fingers."
Blue Racer said, "East Wind, lead Stump to a different village,"
And the Reeds whispered, "Yes!" and the East Wind, "Yes!"

Stump said, "Where are you, Weasel?" searching the swamp
And "Where are you, Magpie?" fighting the tall Reeds
And "Come quick, Blue Racer!" parting the thick stalks,
But the Reeds said, "Hush!" and "Here!" and "Over here!"
And East Wind, weaving, said, "There! Look there!"

Stump trampled the Reeds and swept them down with a stick,
Uprooted them, looked over and under, walked miles
And still saw Reeds and Reeds. He plucked a fistful,
Shouting, "Why have you hidden my People?
They belong to me! You are nothing!"

"Throw stones at me," said East Wind. "Stand where we stand,"
Said the Reeds, "we will keep you, we will listen forever."
"Breathe all of me," said East Wind. "Dream what we dream,"
Said the Reeds. "We too have teeth and wings," said East Wind,
"Come, wear the long quick skin of the moon."

Stump felt afraid. He heard the East Wind whisper,
"Weasel, Magpie, Blue Racer, for all the People,
Asked us to show you how to find your village.
This way! This is the way!" And in the dying evening
Stump entered his dark village, the lodges empty.

HOW STUMP FISHED IN THE BLACK RIVER

Stump said, "I will fish in the Black River."
He stole Black Whale's tooth, sinew from Black Bear,
A branch from Black Locust, and Black Spider's
Longest thread, spun between moon and moon.

But the People said, "No! No one must fish there,
Not even Loon or Fish Hawk. No one knows
What lives under that water." Stump answered,
"I will catch and eat what no one has ever seen."

He called Fish Hawk and Loon. "I will teach you
To scream my name: He-Catches-the-Soul-of-the-River."
From Loon's swift breast, from Fish Hawk's hovering tail
He pulled black feathers and thrust them into his hair.

And he cast his hook far over the current
Where it ran darkest like the river of clouds
From the black throat of North Wind in the winter
And waited, singing, "Now I shall find my power."

He felt his hook hold still. Slowly the thread
Went down and down, slipped through his straining fingers
Sharply and keenly till the end slid under water
Where no one could catch it, then or ever.

And Stump crouched in the shallows, his hands bleeding.

HOW STUMP BECAME ROCK'S BROTHER

Stump walked far, lost in the heat of the day.
Sweating, he sat on Rock and said, "My brother,
You may have my robe." He threw it aside
Over Rock's heavy shoulders and wandered on.

A great cloud blackened the earth. Stump turned
And hurried back to Rock sitting still and dry.
Stump said, "Give me my robe again for the rain."
Rock whispered through the robe, "Now it is mine."

"You have no need of a robe," Stump said and snatched it
And wrapped it around him, walking into the storm.
But soon, behind, he heard something like thunder
And saw Rock rumbling after him: "Give me my robe!"

Stump ran past Nighthawk, crying, "Help me! Help me!
Rock is chasing us all!" But Nighthawk said, "No.
Rock is my nest. All night I ride on the wind,
All day I sleep on Rock: he is my day-cloud."

Stump ran past Buffalo, crying, "Save me! Save me!
Rock wants to kill us all!" But Buffalo
Said, "No. When the People hunt me, Rock deceives them:
We look the same. He splits their strongest arrows."

Stump ran past Bear, crying, "Only you can help me!
Rock wants to crush us all!" But Bear said, "No.
Rock is the roof of my lodge. He lasts through the Moon
Of the Cracking Trees. He is my winter sky."

Stump stood alone in the rain then, and Rock tumbled
Closer and closer, bumping and booming.
He was no day-cloud. He was no good protector
Against the shafts of the hunting weather.

Kneeling, Stump offered his robe again, and Rock
Halted against his forehead, solid and cold.
"I need no robe," Rock said. "I wear this rain.
Tomorrow I wear the sun or the snow, no matter."

Stump opened his arms and clung to Rock. Rock said,
"I hear your heart. Now you may stand against me.
No one will hunt you. You may sleep beneath me
With or without a robe. Welcome, lost brother."

HOW STUMP DREAMED OF EARTHMAKER

Stump said, "I must dream of Earthmaker."
Three days and nights he fasted and dreamed
Everything under the earth: the melted and lost
Sun of the Stone River, Copper Root, Flint Man
Whose tongue goes straight for the soul, Black Fire
And Slate Bird flying together under granite.

"No!" Stump said. "I must have Earthmaker
Here in my heart's eye." And he dreamed
Everything on the earth: Old Running Moss
And Thorn Foot racing with green shadows,
Skull Cup, Man-Inside-Out hunting his lost thumb,
The claws of Rat shaking the bonebush.

Stump cried, "Earthmaker! Earthmaker! The People say
No one has ever dreamed you." And he dreamed
Everything over the earth: Rainbow Man
Bent high across water, the burning feathers
Of Kingfisher gathered from the Land of the Dead,
Ice Tooth, Broken Cloud, Snake-Falling-Forever,

And went on dreaming into the heart's thicket
Till he saw Raven crack the egg of the sun
And Blue Wolf break the long bones of the moon,
Till he dreamed the five wrong names of Death.
The sky came close and huge. At last, Earthmaker
Loomed over him like the face of the First Darkness.

Stump said, "Now I have dreamed you. Now I look
Into your face. Now you shall make me wise."
And suddenly like a mouth the great mask
Opened, and took him in, and closed its teeth,
And Stump became a dream of Stump
In the heart of Earthmaker whose face no man can know.

4

Songs for the Dream Catchers

SONG FOR THE PAINTING OF THE DEAD

Now, in the black branches
Perched stiff or hanging
With your voices broken,
You have come back, Dead Ones.

Sit crooked at the fire
While I gather the hard knot
Of my heart, as hard as yours,
While I gather the blood of flowers,

The sweat of sky and sun.
Here, with my shaking fingers
I will touch your faces.
I will fill your lost eyes.

Again, you will paint for war.
I will paint the bare bones
With skin as tight as drumskin,
With the loud strokes of Breathmaker.

You will move and sing.
None will go who does not return.
None will be here, Dead Ones,
Who has not been yours.

SONG FOR THE EATING OF BARNACLES

I carry the stones you cling to
And heap them ashore.
Sharp, white-clustered Barnacles,
Teeth of Salt Woman, forgive me:
I must make you a flat house
Out of sticks and eel grass
And set it on fire.

Now over the mud-flats
I call the chalky smoke
To loosen your chalk roots.
You must fall out of the tide's jaw
To sleep in my basket,
Then dream of the feast
Where I will taste your secret.

Do not be afraid: my teeth
Will close against your teeth,
Pale and hard as yours.
I do what you have done
In the swelling and shrinking water,
What you will do again when I throw you
Back to gray Sea Mother.

SONG FOR THE STEALING OF A SPRING

This place where water grows
Out of stone, under willows,
Where the ax of the moon falls,
Cut-by-the-Halfmoon-Spring,
Come, my people are waiting.

They have dreamed you.
I must gather you gently
In my robe for a night's journey.
Do not be afraid when Horned Owl
Shakes his mouse-rattle.

I will carry you, Spring-No-One-Has-Tasted.
I will plant you in this dry season
Where you will grow green and cold.
I, the dream-catcher Only One,
I will do it, Rainbush, Rainskin.

SONG FOR SNAKE

Come out of your coil in the yellow shadow
Low under the mesquite.
Lie still in the sunlight.
I will spread my robe to hold you.

Here over your barbed tongue, Long Brother,
I shake the gray-spotted buzzard feather:
Now stare your anger away without eyelids.
Lower the ghost's backbone of your rattle.

High in my house against rocks all year,
I have waited for your coming.
Deep in your house among rocks all winter,
You have waited for my song.

We must draw the clouds together.
If I hold you over my head where my soul sits,
You will see where the rain is hiding
From our crackling roots.

If I feel your teeth, no matter.
Do the clouds not strike the earth over and over
With fire like yours? Are we not still here?
Call down the striking weather.

SONG AGAINST THE SKY

What is wrong with Sky?
Look, he is crumbling fire
Over the white river.
He is spilling all the stars
Out of the horn spoon
To hiss in the ocean.
He is shattering, shattering
The ice of his heart
And flinging the pieces here
To splinter the last alder.
He has cut the moon
In half, and again in half
To be skinned and eaten.
We must make war
Against this cracking Sky
Soon or be broken:
He has broken the post of heaven.

SONG FOR A STOLEN SOUL

Sky, I am standing
Beneath your bitter morning,
Holding my song
Shut like a hawk's wing.

Sky, you know
I can fly above you.
I can split the skull of Rainbow,
Scatter the ashes of snow.

You know Four Winds would come
Now if I called them,
Even the Second Moon
If I spoke its true name.

I will not wait for darkness
Again to climb to your house.
Here in your blue face
The wing of my song stretches.

Sky, now you will break
At the first swift stroke
Of my song's beak.
Give my soul back!

SONG FOR THE SKULL OF BLACK BEAR

You came out of pity for my empty mouth
And the wind over my shoulders
As heavy as your paws.
We stood against each other
In the Dance of the Torn Bellies,
But your robe, even without you,
Was heavier than I could carry.
Hung from my neck, your claws
Have shamed my fingers.

Once I was a true hunter
Afraid to speak your name—
Blue Tongue, Old Crooked Foot,
Wearer of the mask Many Bees,
Tree Carver, Honey Snout,
Stands-Like-a-Man, Snow Sleeper
With breath the color of ghosts.
Now I must join you. Now I say
Black Bear, Black Bear.

I have blackened my face
To be your skin, to honor
The thin blood I must give you.
Like your skull in the thick woods
You will hide in the thick of my sleep.
I will dream you and your jaws.
In the Moon of Half-ripeness
You will redden your face to mourn me
When my skull lies by yours.

SONG FOR THE BONES OF SALMON

I have counted your bones,
Salmon, my sister,
Even the thin gillbones
Like the nets of Spider.
Only a few are broken.
Let this song be those bones.

Let it be the scales lost
On the hard stones
Where you strained at nesting.
Let my song be your cupped eye
Where the flies have come for days
As if to the last spring.

Let it be your flesh,
The long muscles stronger
Than the white water.
Let my song fill your mouth
Like your own strange breath,
The wind inside the river.

Now go downstream swiftly,
Your mouth to its mouth.
Take my song into the salt.
Feed long, feed for us both,
And I will wait gladly
Till you come again to die.

SONG FOR ICE

Ice, I ask for nothing
From the nine spirits
Between Ice-Dying
And Ice-Being-Born:
If you wish to crack
As deep as Earthmaker,
Or burst into rainbows
Under my slit eyes
Peering through whalebone,
Or heave in slabs,
Or bulge into clouds
Harder than ax-heads,
Or turn to a crooked sky
Where Snow Goose and Bear
Can neither swim nor stand,
Or be Ice-Clear, Ice-Hollow,
Ice-White-With-Anger,
Or Ice-Groaning-With-Hunger,
You will do as you please.

If you drift in the night,
Turning your floes around
Under my dreaming feet
Till every step takes back
A step of my journey,
I will not sing against you.
Ice, we must bear each other.
Have we not frozen together
In the long darkness
And stretched in the same weather
As hard and cold as brothers?
Will we not shrink, then turn
To the same wild water?